T0219718

Lecture Notes in Computer Science   **8759**

Commenced Publication in 1973
Founding and Former Series Editors:
Gerhard Goos, Juris Hartmanis, and Jan van Leeuwen

More information about this series at http://www.springer.com/series/7407

Stefano Markidis · Erwin Laure (Eds.)

Solving Software Challenges for Exascale

International Conference
on Exascale Applications and Software,
EASC 2014
Stockholm, Sweden, April 2–3, 2014
Revised Selected Papers

 Springer

Editors
Stefano Markidis
KTH Royal Institute of Technology
Stockholm
Sweden

Erwin Laure
KTH Royal Institute of Technology
Stockholm
Sweden

ISSN 0302-9743   ISSN 1611-3349   (electronic)
Lecture Notes in Computer Science
ISBN 978-3-319-15975-1   ISBN 978-3-319-15976-8   (eBook)
DOI 10.1007/978-3-319-15976-8

Library of Congress Control Number: 2015932683

LNCS Sublibrary: SL1 – Theoretical Computer Science and General Issues

Springer Cham Heidelberg New York Dordrecht London

Printed on acid-free paper

Springer International Publishing AG Switzerland is part of Springer Science+Business Media
(www.springer.com)

Preface

Exascale supercomputers will deliver an unprecedented computing power of 10^{18} floating point operations per second through extreme parallelism likely achieved from hybrid computer architectures. Software and scientific applications running on exascale supercomputer face the challenge of effectively exploiting this computing power. To address this challenge, many potentially disruptive changes are needed in software and applications. The Exascale Applications and Software Conference (EASC) brings together all developers and researchers involved in solving the software challenges of the exascale era. This volume collected selected contributions from the second EASC in Stockholm during April 2–3, 2014. The volume is intended for use by researchers and students of computer science and computational physics. In particular, the volume is very well suited for use by developers of parallel codes, new programming models, run-time systems, and tools for petascale and exascale supercomputers.

This volume is organized into two parts. The first series of articles presents the new developments and algorithms in large scientific applications from different scientific domains, such as biochemistry, computational fluid dynamics, and neutronics. In particular, these articles show how to exploit different levels of parallelism (vector instructions, intra-node and inter-node levels) on hybrid supercomputers in the molecular dynamics GROMACS and computational fluid dynamics Nek5000 codes. Innovative algorithms for reducing memory storage in Monte Carlo methods for neutronics and for improving the quality of sparse domain decomposition in lattice-Boltzmann methods are presented. The second part of the volume presents advancements in software development environments for exascale. The performance modeling of the HPX-5 run-time system for the LULESH proxy application is presented and the co-design work is explained. One article analyzes the effect of system noise on distributed applications at large scale. The new developments in the MUST MPI correctness checker and the VAMPIR performance monitoring tool are presented. Finally, an article on the Vistle visualization tool for distributed environments concludes the volume.

January 2015   Stefano Markidis

Organization

EASC 2014 was organized by the European Commission funded projects CRESTA (Grant Agreement No. 287703, cresta-project.eu), EPiGRAM (Grant Agreement No. 610598, epigram-project.eu), and by the Swedish e-Science Research Center SeRC (e-science.se)

Steering Group

Erwin Laure	KTH Royal Institute of Technology, Sweden
Stefano Markidis	KTH Royal Institute of Technology, Sweden
William D. Gropp	University of Illinois at Urbana–Champaign, USA
Mark Parsons	EPCC, University of Edinburgh, Scotland, UK
Lorna Smith	EPCC, University of Edinburgh, Scotland, UK
Bastian Koller	HLRS, Germany

Program Committee

Erwin Laure	KTH Royal Institute of Technology, Sweden
Stefano Markidis	KTH Royal Institute of Technology, Sweden
William D. Gropp	University of Illinois, USA
Satoshi Matsuoka	Tokyo Institute of Technology, Japan
Mark Parsons	EPCC, University of Edinburgh, Scotland, UK
Lorna Smith	EPCC, University of Edinburgh, Scotland, UK
Daniel Holmes	EPCC, University of Edinburgh, Scotland, UK
Bastian Koller	HLRS, Germany
Pavan Balaji	Argonne National Laboratory, USA
Jed Brown	Argonne National Laboratory, USA
Robert Clay	Sandia National Laboratories, USA
Roberto Gioiosa	Pacific Northwest National Laboratory, USA
Katie Antypas	NERSC, USA
Leroy Drummond-Lewis	Lawrence Berkeley National Laboratory, USA
Alec Johnson	Katholieke Universiteit Leuven, Belgium

Sponsoring Institutions

Cray Inc., Seattle, WA, USA
Mellanox Technologies, Sunnyvale, CA, USA

Contents

Towards Exascale
Scientific Applications

Tackling Exascale Software Challenges in Molecular Dynamics Simulations with GROMACS

Szilárd Páll[1], Mark James Abraham[1], Carsten Kutzner[2], Berk Hess[1], and Erik Lindahl[1,3](✉)

[1] Department of Theoretical Biophysics, Science for Life Laboratory, KTH Royal Institute of Technology, 17121 Solna, Sweden
`erik.lindahl@scilifelab.se`
[2] Theoretical and Computational Biophysics Department, Max Planck Institute for Biophysical Chemistry, Am Fassberg 11, 37077 Göttingen, Germany
[3] Department of Biochemistry & Biophysics, Center for Biomembrane Research, Stockholm University, 10691 Stockholm, Sweden

Abstract. GROMACS is a widely used package for biomolecular simulation, and over the last two decades it has evolved from small-scale efficiency to advanced heterogeneous acceleration and multi-level parallelism targeting some of the largest supercomputers in the world. Here, we describe some of the ways we have been able to realize this through the use of parallelization on all levels, combined with a constant focus on absolute performance. Release 4.6 of GROMACS uses SIMD acceleration on a wide range of architectures, GPU offloading acceleration, and both OpenMP and MPI parallelism within and between nodes, respectively. The recent work on acceleration made it necessary to revisit the fundamental algorithms of molecular simulation, including the concept of neighborsearching, and we discuss the present and future challenges we see for exascale simulation - in particular a very fine-grained task parallelism. We also discuss the software management, code peer review and continuous integration testing required for a project of this complexity.

1 Introduction

Molecular Dynamics simulation of biological macromolecules has evolved from a narrow statistical-mechanics method into a widely applied biophysical research tool that is used outside theoretical chemistry. Supercomputers are now as important as centrifuges or test tubes in chemistry. However, this success also considerably raises the bar for molecular simulation implementations - it is no longer sufficient to reproduce experimental results or e.g. show proof-of-concept relative scaling. To justify the substantial supercomputing resources required by many computational chemistry projects the most important focus today is simply absolute simulation performance and the scientific results achieved. Exascale

---

The authors 'S. Páll and M.J. Abraham' contributed equally.

© Springer International Publishing Switzerland 2015
S. Markidis and E. Laure (Eds.): EASC 2014, LNCS 8759, pp. 3–27, 2015.
DOI: 10.1007/978-3-319-15976-8_1

computing has potential to take simulation to new heights, but the combination of challenges that face software preparing for deployment at the exascale to deliver these results are unique in the history of software. The days of simply buying new hardware with a faster clock rate and getting shorter times to solution with old software are gone. The days of running applications on a single core are gone. The days of heterogeneous processor design to suit floating-point computation are back again. The days of performance being bounded by the time taken for floating-point computations are ending fast. The need to design with multi-core and multi-node parallelization in mind at all points is here to stay, which also means Amdahl's law [3] is more relevant than ever.[1]

A particular challenge for biomolecular simulations is that the computational problem size is fixed by the geometric size of the protein and the atomic-scale resolution of the model physics. Most life science problems can be reduced to this size (or smaller). It is possible to simulate much larger systems, but it is typically not relevant. Second, the timescale of dynamics involving the entire system increases much faster than the length scale, due to the requirement of sampling the exponentially larger number of ensemble microstates. This means that weak scaling is largely irrelevant for life science; to make use of increasing amounts of computational resources to simulate these systems, we have to rely either on strong-scaling software engineering techniques, or ensemble simulation techniques.

The fundamental algorithm of molecular dynamics assigns positions and velocities to every particle in the simulation system, and specifies the model physics that governs the interactions between particles. The forces can then be computed, which can be used to update the positions and velocities via Newton's second law, using a given finite time step. This numerical integration scheme is iterated a large number of times, and it generates a series of samples from the thermodynamic ensemble defined by the model physics. From these samples, observations can be made that confirm or predict experiment. Typical model physics have many components to describe the different kinds of bonded and non-bonded interactions that exist. The *non-bonded interactions* between particles model behaviour like van der Waals forces, or Coulomb's law. The non-bonded interactions are the most expensive aspects of computing the forces, and the subject of a very large amount of research, computation and optimization.

Historically, the GROMACS molecular dynamics simulation suite has aimed at being a general-purpose tool for studying biomolecular systems, such as shown in Fig. 1. The development of the simulation engine focused heavily on maximizing single-core floating-point performance of its innermost compute kernels for non-bonded interactions. These kernels typically compute the electrostatic and van der Waals forces acting on each simulation particle from its interactions with all other inside a given spherical boundary. These kernels were first written in C,

---

[1] Amdahl's law gives a model for the expected (and maximum) speedup of a program when parallelized over multiple processors with respect to the serial version. It states that the achievable speedup is limited by the sequential part of the program.

then FORTRAN, and later optimized in assembly language, mostly for commodity x86-family processors, because the data dependencies of the computations in the kernels were too challenging for C or FORTRAN compilers (then or now). The kernels were also specialized for interactions within and between water molecules, because of the prevalence of such interactions in biomolecular simulations. From one point-of-view, this extensive use of interaction-specific kernels can be seen as a software equivalent of application-specific integrated circuits.

Recognizing the need to build upon this good work by coupling multiple processors, GROMACS 4.0 [14] introduced a minimal-communication neutral territory domain-decomposition (DD) algorithm, [7,8] with fully dynamic load balancing. This spatial decomposition of the simulation volume created high-level data parallelism that was effective for near-linear scaling of the computation at around 400 atoms per core. The DD implementation required the use of MPI for message-passing parallel constructs. However, the needs of many simulation users can be met within a single node, [23] and in that context the implementation overhead of MPI libraries was too high, not to mention it is difficult to employ in distributed computing. In GROMACS 4.5, [20] we implemented a multi-threaded MPI library with the necessary subset of the MPI API. The library has both POSIX and Windows threads back-ends (hence called thread-MPI) and uses highly efficient hardware-supported atomic and lock-free synchronization primitives. This allows the existing DD implementation to work across multiple cores of a single node without depending on any external MPI library.

However, the fundamental limitation remained of a one-to-one mapping of MPI ranks to cores, and to domains. On the one hand, there is always a limit to how small a spatial domain can be, which will limit the number of domains the simulation box can be decomposed into, which in turn limits the number of cores that a parallelization with such a mapping can utilize. On the other hand, the one-to-one domains to cores mapping is cache-friendly as it creates independent data sets so that cores sharing caches can act without conflict, but the size of the volume of data that must be communicated so that neighboring domains act coherently grows rapidly with the number of domains. This approach is only scalable for a fixed problem size if the latency of communication between all cores is comparable and the communication book-keeping overhead grows only linearly with the number of cores. Neither is true, because network latencies are orders of magnitude higher than shared-cache latencies. This is clearly a major problem for designing for the exascale, where many cores, many nodes and non-uniform memory and communication latencies will be key attributes.

The other important aspect of the target simulations for designing for strong scaling is treating the long-range components of the atomic interactions. Many systems of interest are spatially heterogeneous on the nanometer scale (e.g. proteins embedded in membranes and solvated in water), and the simulation artefacts caused by failing to treat the long-range effects are well known. The *de facto* standard for treating the long-range electrostatic interactions has become the smooth particle-mesh Ewald (PME) method, [12] whose cost for N atoms

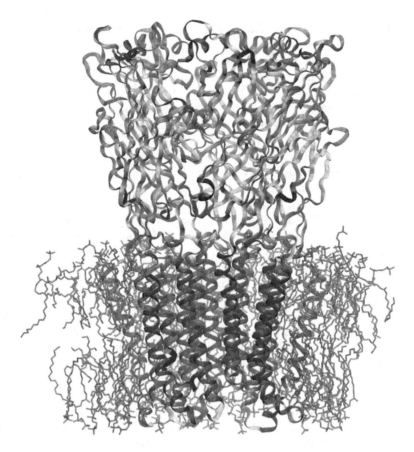

Fig. 1. A typical GROMACS simulation system, featuring the ligand-gated ion-channel membrane protein GLIC (colored), embedded in a lipid membrane (grey). The whole system is solvated in water (not shown), giving a total of around 145,000 atoms. Image created with VMD [15] (Colour figure online).

scales as $N \log(N)$. A straightforward implementation where each rank of a parallel computation participates in an equivalent way leads to a 3D Fast Fourier Transform (FFT) that communicates globally. This communication quickly limits the strong scaling. To mitigate this, GROMACS 4.0 introduced a multiple-program multiple-data (MPMD) implementation that dedicates some ranks to the FFT part; now only those ranks do all-to-all FFT communication. GROMACS 4.5 improved further by using a 2D pencil decomposition [11,16] in reciprocal space, within the same MPMD implementation. This coarse-grained task parallelism works well on machines with homogeneous hardware, but it is harder to port to accelerators or combine with RDMA constructs.

The transformation of GROMACS needed to perform well on exascale-level parallel hardware began after GROMACS 4.5. This requires radical algorithm changes, and better use of parallelization constructs from the ground up, not as an afterthought. More hands are required to steer the project, and yet the old functionality written before their time must generally be preserved. Computer architectures are evolving rapidly, and no single developer can know the details of all of them. In the following sections we describe how we are addressing some of these challenges, and our ongoing plans for addressing others.

2   Handling Exascale Software Challenges: Algorithms and Parallelization Schemes

2.1   Multi-level Parallelism

Modern computer hardware is not only parallel, but exposes multiple levels of parallelism depending on the type and speed of data access and communication capabilities across different compute elements. For a modern superscalar CPU such as Intel Haswell, even a single core is equipped with 8 different execution ports, and it is not even possible to buy a single-core chip. Add hardware threads, complex communication crossbars, memory hierarchies, and caches larger than hard disks from the 1990s. This results in a complex hierarchical organization of compute and communication/network elements from SIMD units and caches to network topologies, each level in the hierarchy requiring a different type of software parallelization for efficient use. HPC codes have traditionally focused on only two levels of parallelism: intra-node and inter-node. Such codes typically rely solely on MPI parallelization to target parallelism on multiple levels: both intra-socket, intra-node, and inter-node. This approach had obvious advantages before the multi-core and heterogeneous computing era when improvements came from CPU frequency scaling and evolution of interconnect. However, nowadays most scientific problems require complex parallel software architecture to be able use petaflop hardware efficiently and going toward exascale this is becoming a necessity. This is particularly true for molecular dynamics which requires reducing the wall-time per iteration to improve simulation performance.

On the lowest level, processors typically contain SIMD (single instruction multiple data) units which offer fine-grained data-parallelism through silicon dedicated to executing a limited set of instructions on multiple, currently typically 4–16, data elements simultaneously. Exploiting this low-level and fine-grained parallelism has become crucial for achieving high performance, especially with new architectures like AVX and Intel MIC supporting wide SIMD. One level higher, multi-core CPUs have become the standard and several architectures support multiple hardware threads per core. Hence, typical multi-socket SMP machines come with dozens of cores capable of running 2–4 threads each (through simultaneous multi-threading, SMT, support). Simply running multiple processes (MPI ranks) on each core or hardware thread is typically less efficient than multi-threading. Achieving strong scaling in molecular dynamics requires efficient use of the cache hierarchy, which makes the picture even more complex. On the other hand, a chip cannot be considered a homogeneous cluster either. Accelerator coprocessors like GPUs or Intel MIC, often referred to as many-core, add another layer of complexity to the intra-node parallelism. These require fine-grained parallelism and carefully tuned data access patterns, as well as special programming models. Current accelerator architectures like GPUs also add another layer of interconnect in form of PCIe bus (Peripheral Component Interconnect Express) as well as a separate main memory. This means that data movement across the PCIe link often limits overall throughput. Integration of traditional latency-oriented CPU cores with throughput-oriented cores like those in GPUs or MIC accelerators is ongoing, but the cost of data movement between the different units will at least for the foreseeable future be a factor that needs to be optimized for.

Typical HPC hardware exhibits non-uniform memory access (NUMA) behavior on the node level: accessing data from different CPUs or cores of CPUs has a non-uniform cost. We started multithreading trials quite early with the idea of easily achieving load balancing, but the simultaneous introduction of NUMA suddenly meant a processor resembled a cluster internally. Indiscriminately accessing memory across NUMA nodes will frequently lead to performance that is lower than for MPI. Moreover, the NUMA behavior extends to other compute and communication components: the cost of communicating with an accelerator or through a network interface typically depends on the intra-node bus topology and requires special attention. On the top level, the interconnect links together compute nodes into a network topology. A side-effect of the multi-core evolution is that, while the network capacity (latency and bandwidth) per compute node has improved, the typical number of CPU cores they serve has increased faster; the capacity available per core has decreased substantially.

In order to exploit the capabilities of each level of hardware parallelism, a performance-oriented application needs to consider multiple levels of parallelism: SIMD parallelism for maximizing single-core/thread performance; multithreading to exploit advantages of multi-core and SMT (e.g. fast data sharing); inter-node communication-based parallelism (e.g. message passing with MPI); and heterogeneous parallelism by utilizing both CPUs and accelerators like GPUs.

Driven by this evolution of hardware, we have initiated a re-redesign of the parallelization in GROMACS. In particular, recent efforts have focused on improvements targeting all levels of parallelization: new algorithms for wide SIMD and accelerator architectures, a portable and extensible SIMD parallelization framework, efficient multi-threading throughout the entire code, and an asynchronous offload-model for accelerators. The resulting multi-level parallelization scheme implemented in GROMACS 4.6 is illustrated in Fig. 2. In the following sections, we will give an overview of these improvements, highlighting the advances they provide in terms of making efficient use of current petascale hardware, as well as in paving the road towards exascale computing.

2.2 SIMD Parallelism

All modern CPU and GPU architectures use SIMD-like instructions to achieve high flop rates. Any computational code that aims for high performance will have to make use of SIMD. For very regular work, such as matrix-vector multiplications, the compiler can generate good SIMD code, although manually tuned vendor libraries typically do even better. But for irregular work, such as short-range particle-particle non-bonded interactions, the compiler usually fails since it cannot control data structures. If you think your compiler is really good at optimizing, it can be an eye-opening experience to look at the raw assembly instructions actually generated. In GROMACS, this was reluctantly recognized a decade ago and SSE and Altivec SIMD kernels were written manually in assembly. These kernels were, and still are, extremely efficient for interactions involving water molecules, but other interactions do not parallelize well with SIMD using the standard approach of unrolling a particle-based Verlet-list [25].

It is clear that a different approach is needed in order to use wide SIMD execution units like AVX or GPUs. We developed a novel approach, where particles are grouped into spatial clusters containing fixed number of particles [17]. First, the particles are placed on a grid in the x and y dimensions, and then binned in the z dimension. This efficiently groups particles that are close in space, and permits the construction of a list of clusters, each containing exactly M particles. A list is then constructed of all those cluster pairs containing particles that may

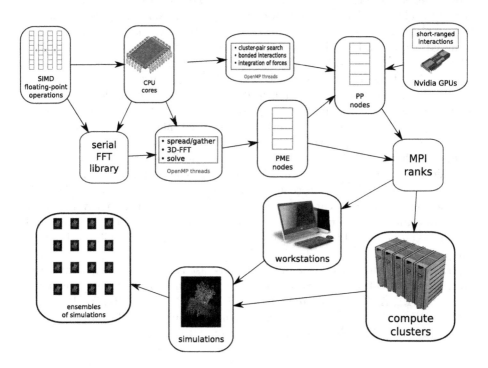

Fig. 2. Illustration of multi-level parallelism in GROMACS 4.6. This exploits several kinds of fine-grained data parallelism, a multiple-program multiple-data (MPMD) decomposition separating the short-range particle-particle (PP) and long-range Particle Mesh Ewald (PME) force calculation algorithms, coarse-grained data parallelism with domain-decomposition (DD) over MPI ranks (implemented either on single-node workstations or compute clusters), and ensembles of related simulations scheduled e.g. by a distributed computing controller.

be close enough to interact. This list of pairs of interacting clusters is reused over multiple successive evaluations of the non-bonded forces. The list is constructed with a buffer to prevent particle diffusion corrupting the implementation of the model physics.

The kernels that implement the computation of the interactions between two clusters i and j use SIMD load instructions to fill vector registers with copies of the positions of all M particles in i. The loop over the N particles in j is unrolled according to the SIMD width of the CPU. Inside this loop, SIMD load instructions fill vector registers with positions of all N particles from the j cluster. This permits the computation of N interactions between an i and all j particles simultaneously, and the computation of $M \times N$ interactions in the inner loop without needing to load particle data. With wide SIMD units it is efficient to process more than one j cluster at a time.

M, N and the number of j clusters to process can be adjusted to suit the underlying characteristics of the hardware. Using $M = 1$ and $N = 1$ recovers the original Verlet-list algorithm. On CPUs, GROMACS uses $M = 4$ and $N = 2$, 4 or 8, depending on the SIMD width. On NVIDIA GPUs, we use $M = 8$ and $N = 4$ to calculate 32 interactions at once with 32 hardware threads executing in lock-step. To further improve the ratio of arithmetic to memory operations when using GPUs, we add another level of hierarchy by grouping 8 clusters together. Thus we store 64 particles in shared memory and calculate interactions with about half of these for every particle in the cluster-pair list.

The kernel implementations reach about 50 % of the peak flop rate on all supported hardware, which is very high for MD. This comes at the cost of calculating about twice as many interactions as required; not all particle pairs in all cluster pairs will be within the cut-off at each time step, so many interactions are computed that are known to produce a zero result. The extra zero interactions can actually be put to use as an effective additional pair list buffer additionally to the standard Verlet list buffer. As we have shown here, this scheme is flexible, since N and M can be adapted to current and future hardware. Most algorithms and optimization tricks that have been developed for particle-based pair lists can be reused for the cluster-pair list, although many will not improve the performance.

The current implementation of the cluster-based non-bonded algorithm already supports a wide range of SIMD instruction sets and accelerator architectures: SSE2, SSE4.1, AVX (256-bit and 128-bit with FMA), AVX2, BG/Q QPX, Intel MIC (LRBni), NVIDIA CUDA. An implementation on a field-programmable gate array (FPGA) architecture is in progress.

Multi-threaded Parallelism.

Before GROMACS 4.6, we relied mostly on MPI for both inter-node and intra-node parallelization over CPU cores. For MD this has worked well, since there is little data to communicate and at medium to high parallelization all data fits in L2 cache. Our initial plans were to only support OpenMP parallelization in the separate Particle Mesh Ewald (PME) MPI ranks. The reason for using OpenMP in PME was to reduce the number of MPI ranks involved in the costly collective communication for the FFT grid transpose. This 3D-FFT is the only part of the code that involves global data dependencies. Although this indeed greatly reduced the MPI communication cost, it also introduced significant overhead.

GROMACS 4.6 was designed to use OpenMP in all compute-intensive parts of the MD algorithm.[2] Most of the algorithms are straightforward to parallelize using OpenMP. These scale very well, as Fig. 3 shows. Cache-intensive parts of the code like performing domain decomposition, or integrating the forces and velocities show slightly worse scaling. Moreover, the scaling in these parts tends to deteriorate with increasing number of threads in an MPI rank – especially with large number of threads in a rank, and when teams of OpenMP threads cross NUMA boundaries. When simulating at high ratios of cores/particles, each MD step can take as little as a microsecond. There are many OpenMP barriers used in the many code paths that are parallelized with OpenMP, each of which takes a few microseconds, which can be costly.

Accordingly, the hybrid MPI + OpenMP parallelization is often slower than an MPI-only scheme as Fig. 3 illustrates. Since PP (particle-particle) ranks only do low-volume local communication, the reduction in MPI communication from using the hybrid scheme is apparent only at high parallelization. There, MPI-only parallelization (e.g. as in GROMACS 4.5) puts a hard upper limit on the number of cores that can be used, due to algorithmic limits on the spatial domain size, or the need to communicate with more than one nearest neighbor. With the hybrid scheme, more cores can operate on the same spatial domain assigned to an MPI rank, and there is no longer a hard limit on the parallelization. Strong scaling curves now extend much further, with a more gradual loss of parallel efficiency. An example is given in Fig. 4, which shows a membrane protein system scaling to twice as many cores with hybrid parallelization and reach double the peak performance of GROMACS 4.5. In some cases, OpenMP-only parallelization can be much faster than MPI-only parallelization if the load for each stage of the force computation can be balanced individually. A typical example is a solute in solvent, where the solute has bonded interactions but the solvent does not. With OpenMP, the bonded interactions can be distributed equally over all threads in a straightforward manner.

Heterogeneous Parallelization.

Heterogeneous architectures combine multiple types of processing units, typically latency- and throughput-oriented cores – most often CPUs and accelerators like GPUs, Intel MIC, or FPGAs. Many-core accelerator architectures have been become increasingly popular in technical and scientific computing mainly due to their impressive raw floating point performance. However, in order to efficiently utilize these architectures, a very high level of fine-grained parallelism is required.

---

[2] At the time of that decision, sharing a GPU among multiple MPI ranks was inefficient, so the only efficient way to use multiple cores in a node was with OpenMP within a rank. This constraint has since been relaxed.

The massively parallel nature of accelerators, in particular GPUs, is both an advantage as well as a burden on the programmer. Since not all tasks are well suited for execution on the accelerators this often leads to additional challenges for workload distribution and load balancing. Moreover, current heterogeneous architectures typically use a slow PCIe bus to connect the hardware elements like CPUs and GPUs and move data between the separate global memory of each. This means that explicit data management is required. This adds a further latency overhead to challenge algorithms like MD that already face this as a parallelization bottle-neck.

GPU accelerators were first supported experimentally in GROMACS with the OpenMM library, [10] which was used as a black box to execute the entire simulation on the GPU. This meant that only a fraction of the diverse set of GROMACS algorithms were supported and simulations were limited to single-GPU use. Additionally, while OpenMM offered good performance for implicit-solvent models, the more common type of runs showed little speedup (and in

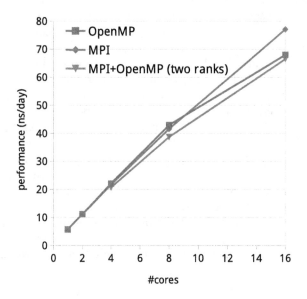

Fig. 3. Comparison of single-node simulation performance using MPI, OpenMP, and combined MPI+OpenMP parallelization. The OpenMP multi-threading (blue) achieves the highest performance and near linear scaling up to 8 threads. It only deteriorates when threads on OpenMP regions need to communicate across the system bus. In contrast, the MPI-only runs (red) that require less communication scale well across sockets. Combining MPI and OpenMP parallelization with two ranks and varying the number of threads (green) results in worse performance due to the added overhead of the two parallelization schemes. Simulations were carried out on a dual-socket node with 8-core Intel Xeon E5-2690 (2.9 GHz Sandy Bridge). Input system: RNAse protein solvated in a rectangular box, 24k atoms, PME electrostatics, 0.9 nm cut-off (Colour figure online).

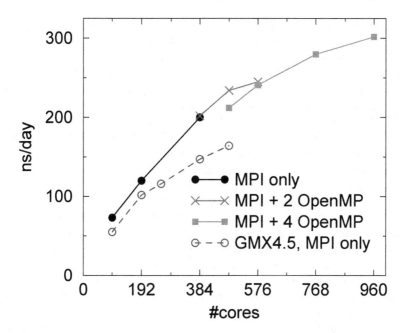

Fig. 4. Improvements in strong scaling performance since GROMACS 4.5, using the $M \times N$ kernels and OpenMP parallelization in GROMACS 4.6. The plot shows simulation performance in ns/day for different software versions and parallelization schemes. Performance with one core per MPI rank is shown for GROMACS 4.5 (purple) and 4.6 (black). Performance with GROMACS 4.6 is shown using two (red) and four (green) cores per MPI rank using OpenMP threading within each MPI rank. Simulations were carried out on the Triolith cluster at NSC, using two 8-core Intel E5-2660 (2.2 GHz Sandy Bridge) processors per node and FDR Infiniband network. The test system is the GLIC membrane protein shown in Fig. 1 (144,000 atoms, PME electrostatics.) (Colour figure online).

some cases slowdown) over the fast performance on multi-core CPUs, thanks to the highly tuned SIMD assembly kernels.

With this experience, we set out to provide native GPU support in GROMACS 4.6 with a few important design principles in mind. Building on the observation that highly optimized CPU code is hard to beat, our goal was to ensure that all compute resources available, both CPU and accelerators, are utilized to the greatest extent possible. We also wanted to ensure that our heterogeneous GPU acceleration supported most existing features of GROMACS in a single code base to avoid having to reimplement major parts of the code for GPU-only execution. This means that the most suitable parallelization is the offload model, which other MD codes have also employed successfully [9,18]. As Fig. 5 illustrates, we aim to execute the compute-intensive short-range non-bonded force calculation on GPU accelerators, while the CPU computes bonded and long-range electrostatics forces, because the latter are communication intensive.

The newly designed future-proof SIMD-oriented algorithm for evaluating non-bonded interactions with accelerator architectures in mind has been discussed already. It is highly efficient at expressing the fine-grained parallelism present in the pair-force calculation. Additionally, the atom cluster-based approach is designed for data reuse which is further emphasized by the super-cluster grouping. As a result, our CUDA implementation is characterized by a high ratio of arithmetic to memory operations which allows avoiding memory bottlenecks. These algorithmic design choices and the extensive performance tuning led to strongly instruction-latency bound CUDA non-bonded kernels, in contrast to most traditional particle-based GPU algorithms which are reported to be memory bound [4,9]. Our CUDA GPU kernels also scale well, reaching peak pair-force throughput already around 20,000 particles per GPU.

In contrast to typical data-parallel programming for homogeneous CPU-only machines, heterogeneous architectures require additional code to manage task scheduling and concurrent execution on the different compute elements, CPU cores and GPUs in the present case. This is a complex component of our heterogeneous parallelization which implements the data- and control-flow with the main goal of maximizing the utilization of both CPU and GPU by ensuring optimal CPU-GPU execution overlap.

We combine a set of CPU cores running OpenMP threads with a GPU. As shown in Fig. 5, the pair-lists required for the non-bonded computation are prepared on the CPU and transferred to the GPU where a pruning step is carried out after which the lists are reused for up to 100 iterations. The extreme floating-point power of GPUs makes it feasible to use the much larger buffers required for this. The transfer of coordinates, charges, and forces as well as compute kernels are launched asynchronously as soon as data becomes available on the CPU. This ensures overlap of CPU and GPU computation. Additional effort has gone into maximizing overlap by reducing the wall-time of CPU-side non-overlapping program parts through SIMD parallelization (in pair search and constraints) and efficient multi-threaded algorithms allowing GROMACS to achieve a typical CPU-GPU overlap of 60–80 %.

This scheme naturally extends to multiple GPUs by using the existing efficient neutral territory domain-decomposition implemented using MPI parallelization. By default, we assign computation on each domain to a single GPU and a set of CPU cores. This typically means decomposing the system into as many domains as GPUs used, and running as many MPI ranks per node as GPUs in the node. However, this will often require to run a large number of OpenMP threads in a rank (8–16 or even more with a single GPU per node), potentially spanning across multiple NUMA domains. As explained in the previous section, this will lead to suboptimal multi-threaded scaling – especially affecting cache-intensive algorithms outside the CPU-GPU overlap region. To avoid this, multiple MPI ranks can share a GPU, which reduces the number of OpenMP threads per rank.

The heterogeneous acceleration in GROMACS delivers 3-4x speedup when comparing CPU only with CPU-GPU runs. Moreover, advanced features like arbitrary simulation box shapes and virtual interaction sites are all supported (Fig. 6). Even though the overhead of managing an accelerator is non-negligible, GROMACS 4.6 shows great strong scaling in GPU accelerated runs reaching 126 atoms/core (1260 atoms/GPU) on common simulation systems (Fig. 7).

Based on a similar parallelization design, the upcoming GROMACS version will also support the Intel MIC accelerator architecture. Intel MIC supports native execution of standard MPI codes using the so-called symmetric mode, where the card is essentially treated as a general-purpose multi-core node. However, as MIC is a highly parallel architecture requiring fine-grained parallelism, many parts of typical MPI codes will be inefficient on these processors. Hence, efficient utilization of Xeon Phi devices in molecular dynamics – especially with typical bio-molecular simulations and strong-scaling in mind – is only possible by treating them as accelerators. Similarly to GPUs, this means a parallelization scheme based on offloading only those tasks that are suitable for wide SIMD and highly thread-parallel execution to MIC.

2.3   Ensemble Simulations

The performance and scaling advances in GROMACS (and many other programs) have made it efficient to run simulations that simply were too large only a few years ago. However, infrastructures such as the European PRACE provide access only to problems that scale to thousands of cores. This used to be an impossible barrier for biomolecular dynamics on anything but ridiculously large systems when an implementation could only run well with hundreds of particles per core. Scaling has improved, but the number of computational units in supercomputers is growing even faster. There are now multiple machines in the world that reach roughly a million cores. Under ideal conditions, GROMACS can scale to levels where each PP rank handles 40 atoms, but there are few if any concrete biological problems that require 40 million atoms without corresponding increases in the number of samples generated. Even in the theoretical case where we could improve scaling to the point where each core only contains a single atom, the simulation system would still be almost an order of magnitude larger than the example in Fig. 1.

To adapt to this reality, researchers are increasingly using large ensembles of simulations, either to simply sample better, or new algorithms such as replica exchange simulation, [24] Markov state models, [22] or milestoning [13] that analyze and exchange data between multiple simulations to improve overall sampling. In many cases, this achieves as much as two-fold superscaling, i.e., an ensemble of 100 simulations running on 10 nodes each might provide the same sampling efficiency as a single simulation running on 2000 cores. To automate this, GROMACS has been co-developed with a new framework for Parallel Adaptive Molecular Dynamics called Copernicus [19]. Given a set of input structures and sampling settings, this framework automatically starts a first batch of sampling runs, makes sure all simulations complete (with extensive support for checkpointing and restarting of failed runs), and automatically performs the adaptive step data analysis to decide what new simulations to start in a second generation. The current ensemble sampling algorithms scale to hundreds

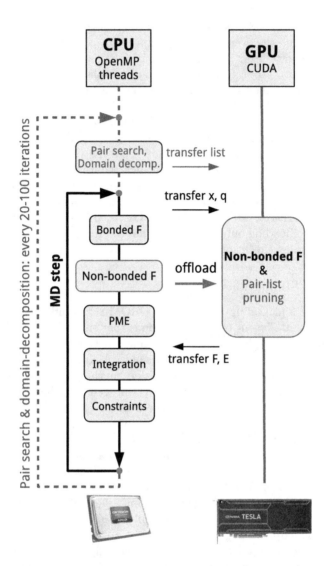

Fig. 5. GROMACS heterogeneous parallelization using both CPU and GPU resources during each simulation time-step. The compute-heavy non-bonded interactions are offloaded to the GPU, while the CPU is responsible for domain-decomposition book-keeping, bonded force calculation, and lattice summation algorithms. The diagram shows tasks carried out during a GPU-accelerated normal MD step (black arrows) as well as a step which includes the additional pair-search and domain-decomposition tasks are carried out (blue arrows). The latter, as shown above in blue, also includes an additional transfer, and the subsequent pruning of the pair list as part of the non-bonded kernel (Colour figure online).

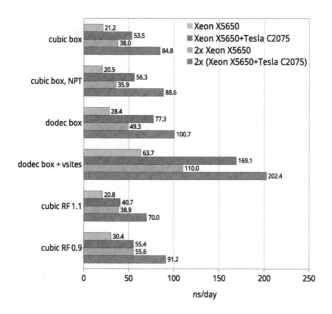

Fig. 6. An important feature of the current heterogeneous GROMACS GPU implementation is that it works, and works efficiently, in combination with most other features of the software. GPU simulations can employ domain decomposition, non-standard boxes, pressure scaling, and virtual interaction sites to significantly improve the absolute simulation performance compared to the baseline. Simulation system: RNAse protein solvated in rectangular (24 K atoms) and rhombic dodecahedron (16.8 k atoms) box, PME electrostatics, cut-off 0.9 nm. Hardware: 2x Intel Xeon E5650 (2.67 GHz Westmere), 2x NVIDIA Tesla C2070 (Fermi) GPU accelerators.

or thousands of parallel simulations (each using up to thousands of cores even for small systems). For the first time in many years, molecular dynamics might actually be able to use all the cores available on next-generation supercomputers rather than constantly being a generation or two behind.

2.4   Multi-level Load Balancing

Achieving strong scaling to a higher core count for a fixed-size problem requires careful consideration of load balance. The advantage provided by spatial DD is one of data locality and reuse, but if the distribution of computational work is not homogeneous then more care is needed. A typical membrane protein simulation is dominated by

- water, which is usually treated with a rigid 3-point model,
- a lipid membrane, whose alkyl tails are modeled by particles with zero partial charge and bonds of constrained length, and
- a protein, which is modeled with a backbone of fixed-length bonds that require a lengthy series of constraint calculations, as well as partial charge on all particles.

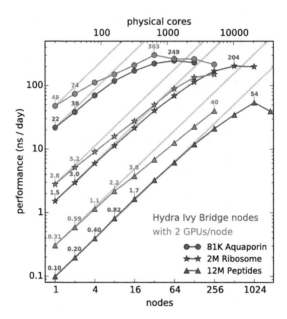

Fig. 7. Strong scaling of GROMACS 4.6 on the HYDRA heterogeneous GPU-equipped machine in Garching, Germany. Grey lines indicate linear scaling. The hybrid version of GROMACS scales very well and achieves impressive absolute performance for both small and large systems. For the smaller systems, peak performance is achieved with 150 atoms per core, and the larger systems achieve sustained effective flop rate of 0.2 petaflops (only counting the number of useful floating-point operations, not the total). Simulation systems: typical production systems of 81 k atoms (circles), 2 M atoms (stars), and 12 M atoms (triangles) in size. Hardware (per node): 2 10-core Xeon E5-2680v2 (2.8 GHz Ivy Bridge), 2 NVIDIA K20X, InfiniBand FDR14 (4×14 Gb/s) network.

These problems are well known, and are addressed in the GROMACS DD scheme via automatic dynamic load balancing that distributes the spatial volumes unevenly according to the observed imbalance in compute load. This approach has limitations because it works at the level of DD domains that must map to MPI ranks, so cores within the same node or socket have unnecessary copies of the same data. We have not yet succeeded in developing a highly effective intra-rank decomposition of work to multiple cores. We hope to address this via intra-node or intra-socket task parallelism.

One advantage of the PME algorithm as implemented in GROMACS is that it is possible to shift the computational workload between the real- and reciprocal-space parts of the algorithm at will. This makes it possible to write code that can run optimally at different settings on different kinds of hardware. The performance of the compute, communication and bookkeeping parts of the overall algorithm vary greatly with the characteristics of the hardware that implements it, and with the properties of the simulation system studied. For example, shifting compute work from reciprocal to real space to make better use of an idle GPU increases the volume that must be communicated during DD, while lowering the required communication volume during the 3D FFTs. Evaluating how best to manage these compromises can only happen at runtime.

The MPMD version of PME is intended to reduce the overall communication cost on typical switched networks by minimizing the number of ranks participating in the 3D FFTs. This requires generating a mapping between PME and non-PME ranks and scheduling data transfer to and from them. However, on hardware with relatively efficient implementations of global communication, it can be advantageous to prefer the SPMD implementation because it has more regular communication patterns [2]. The same may be true on architectures with accelerators, because the MPMD implementation makes no use of the accelerators on the PME ranks. The performance of both implementations is limited by lack of overlap of communication and computation.

Attempts to use low-latency partitioned global address space (PGAS) methods that require single-program multiple-data (SPMD) approaches are particularly challenged, because the gain from any decrease in communication latency must also overcome the overall increase in communication that accompanies the MPMD-to-SPMD transition [21]. The advent of implementations of non-blocking collective (NBC) MPI routines is promising if computation can be found to overlap with the background communication. The most straightforward approach would be to revert to SPMD and hope that the increase in total communication cost is offset by the gain in available compute time, however, the available performance is still bounded by the overall cost of the global communication. Finding compute to overlap with the NBC on the MPMD PME ranks is likely to deliver better results. Permitting PME ranks to execute kernels for bonded and/or non-bonded interactions from their associated non-PME ranks is the most straightforward way to achieve this overlap. This is particularly true at the scaling limit, where the presence of bonded interactions is one of the primary problems in balancing the compute load between the non-PME ranks.

The introduction of automatic ensemble computing introduces another layer of decomposition, by which we essentially achieve MSMPMD parallelism: Multiple-simulation (ensemble), multiple-program (direct/lattice space), and multiple-data (domain decomposition).

2.5   Managing the Long-Range Contributions at Exascale

A promising candidate for exascale-level biomolecular simulations is the use of suitable implementations of fast-multipole methods such as ExaFMM [6,27]. At least one implementation of FMM-based molecular dynamics running on 100,000 cores has been reported, [5] but so far the throughput on problems of comparable size is only equivalent to the best PME-based implementations. FMM-based algorithms can deliver linear scaling of communication and computation with both the number of MPI ranks and the number of particles. This linear scaling is expected to be an advantage when increasing the number of processing units in the exascale era. Early tests showed that the iteration times of ExaFMM doing only long-range work and GROMACS 4.6 doing only short-range work on homogeneous systems of the same size were comparable, so we hope we can deploy a working version in the future.

2.6 Fine-Grained Task Parallelism for Exascale

We plan to address some of the exascale-level strong-scaling problems mentioned above through the use of a more fine-grained task parallelism than what is currently possible in GROMACS. Considerable technical challenges remain to convert OpenMP-based data-parallel loop constructs into series of tasks that are coarse enough to avoid spending lots of time scheduling work, and yet fine enough to balance the overall load. Our initial plan is to experiment with the cross-platform Thread Building Blocks (TBB) library, [1] which can coexist with OpenMP and deploy equivalent loop constructs in the early phases of development. Many alternatives exist; those that require the use of custom compilers, runtime environments, or language extensions are unattractive because that increases the number of combinations of algorithm implementations that must be maintained and tested, and compromises the high portability enjoyed by GROMACS.

One particular problem that might be alleviated with fine-grained task parallelism is reducing the cost of the communication required during the integration phase. Polymers such as protein backbones are modeled with fixed-length bonds, with at least two bonds per particle, which leads to coupled constraints that domain decomposition spreads over multiple ranks. Iterating to satisfy those constraints can be a costly part of the algorithm at high parallelism. Because the spatial regions that contain bonded interactions are distributed over many ranks, and the constraint computations cannot begin until after all the forces for their atoms have been computed, the current implementation waits for all forces on all ranks to be computed before starting the integration phase. The performance of post-integration constraint-satisfaction phase is bounded by the latency for the multiple communication stages required. This means that ranks that lack atoms with coupled bonded interactions, such as all those with only water molecules, literally have nothing to do at this stage. In an ideal implementation, such ranks could contribute very early in each iteration to complete all the tasks needed for the forces for the atoms involved in coupled bond constraints. Integration for those atoms could take place while forces for interactions between unrelated atoms are being computed, so that there is computation to do on all nodes while the communication for the constraint iteration takes place. This kind of implementation would require considerably more flexibility in the book-keeping and execution model, which is simply not present today.

3   Handling Exascale Software Challenges: Process and Infrastructure

3.1   Transition from C to C++98

The major part of the GROMACS code base has been around 1–1.5 million lines of C code since version 4.0 (http://www.ohloh.net/p/gromacs). Ideally, software engineering on such moderately large multi-purpose code bases would take place within the context of effective abstractions [26]. For example, someone developing a new integration algorithm should not need to pay any attention to whether the parallelization is implemented by constructs from a threading library (like POSIX threads), a compiler-provided threading layer (like OpenMP), an external message-passing library (like MPI), or remote direct memory access (like SHMEM). Equally, she/he should not need to know whether the kernels that compute the forces they are using as inputs are running on any particular kind of accelerator or CPU. Implementing such abstractions generally costs some developer time, and some compute time. These are necessary evils if the software is to be able to change as new hardware, new algorithms or new implementations emerge.

Considerable progress has been made in modularizing some aspects of the code base to provide effective abstraction layers. For example, once the main MD iteration loop has begun, the programmer does not need to know whether the MPI layer is provided by an external library because the computation is taking place on multiple nodes, or the internal thread-based implementation is working to parallelize the computation on a single node. Portable abstract atomic operations have been available as a side-effect of the thread-MPI development. Integrators receive vectors of positions, velocities and forces without needing to know the details of the kernels that computed the forces. The dozens of non-bonded kernels can make portable SIMD function calls that compile to the correct hardware operations automatically.

However, the size of the top-level function that implements the loop over time steps has remained at about 1800 code and comment lines since 4.0. It remains riddled with special-case conditions, comments, and function calls for different parallelization conditions, integration algorithms, optimization constructs, housekeeping for communication and output, and ensemble algorithms. The function that computes the forces is even worse, now that both the old and new non-bonded kernel infrastructures are supported! The code complexity is necessary for a general-purpose multi-architecture tool like GROMACS. However, needing to be aware of dozens of irrelevant possibilities is a heavy barrier to participation in the project, because it is very difficult to understand all side effects of a change.

To address this, we are in the process of a transition from C99 to C++98 for much of this high-level control code. While we remain alert to the possibility that HPC compilers will not be as effective at compiling C++98 as they are for C99, the impact on execution time of most of this code is negligible and the impact on developer time is considerable.

Our expectation is that the use of virtual function dispatch will eliminate much of the complexity of understanding conditional code (including switch statements over enumerations that must be updated in widely scattered parts of the code), despite a slightly slower implementation of the actual function call. After all, GROMACS has long used a custom vtable-like implementation for runtime dispatch of the non-bonded interaction kernels. Objects managing resources via RAII exploiting compiler-generated destructor calls for doing the right thing will lead to shorter development times and fewer problems because developers have to manage fewer things. Templated container types will help alleviate the burden of manual memory allocation and deallocation. Existing C++ testing and mocking libraries will simplify the process of developing adequate testing infrastructure, and existing task-parallelism support libraries such as Intel TBB [1] will be beneficial.

It is true that some of these objectives could be met by re-writing in more objected-oriented C, but the prospect of off-loading some tedious tasks to the compiler is attractive.

3.2 Best Practices in Open-Source Scientific Software Development

Version control is widely considered necessary for successful software development. GROMACS used CVS in its early days and now uses Git (git clone git://git.gromacs.org/gromacs.git). The ability to trace when behavior changed and find some metadata about why it might have changed is supremely valuable.

Coordinating the information about desires of users and developers, known problems, and progress with current work is an ongoing task that is difficult with a development team scattered around the world and thousands of users who rarely meet. GROMACS uses the Redmine issue-tracking system[3] to discuss feature development, report and discuss bugs, and to monitor intended and actual progress towards milestones. Commits in the git repository are expected to reference Redmine issues where appropriate, which generates automatic HTML cross-references to save people time finding information.

Peer review of scientific research is the accepted gold standard of quality because of the need for specialist understanding to fully appreciate, value, criticize and improve the work. Software development on projects like GROMACS is comparably complex, and our experience has been that peer review has worked well there. Specifically, all proposed changes to GROMACS – even from the core authors – must go through our Gerrit code-review website[4], and receive positive reviews from at least two other developers of suitable experience, before they can be merged. User- and developer-level documentation must be part of the same change. Requiring this review to happen before acceptance has eliminated many problems before they could be felt. It also creates social pressure for people to be active in reviewing others' code, lest they have no karma with which to get their own proposals reviewed. As features are implemented or bugs fixed,

---

[3] http://redmine.gromacs.org.
[4] http://gerrit.gromacs.org.

corresponding Redmine issues are automatically updated. Gerrit also provides a common venue for developers to share work in progress, either privately or publicly.

Testing is one of the least favourite activities of programmers, who would much rather continue being creative in solving new problems. The standard procedure in software engineering is to deploy continuous integration, where each new or proposed change is subjected to a range of automatic tests. In the GRO-MACS project, we use Jenkins[5] to build the project on a wide range of operating systems (MacOS, Windows, flavours of Linux), compilers (GNU, Intel, Microsoft, clang; and several versions of each), and build configurations (MPI, thread-MPI, OpenMP, different kinds of SIMD), and then automatically test the results for correctness. This immediately finds problems such as programmers using POSIX constructs that are not implemented on Windows. Most of our tests detect regressions, where a change in the code leads to an unintended change in behavior. Unfortunately, many of these tests are still structured around executing a whole MD process, which makes it difficult to track down where a problem has occurred, unless the code change is tightly focused. This motivates the discipline of proposing changes that only have one logical effect, and working towards adding module-level testing. New behaviors are expected to be integrated alongside tests of that behavior, so that we continue to build upon the test infrastructure for the future. All tests are required to pass before code changes can be merged.

Testing regularly for changes in execution speed is an unsolved problem that is particularly important for monitoring our exascale software developments. It is less suited for deployment via continuous integration, because of the quantity of computation required to test the throughput of code like GROMACS with proper load-balancing, at-scale, and on a range of hardware and input conditions. It would be good to be able to execute a weekly end-to-end test run that shows that unplanned performance regressions have not emerged, but we have not prioritized it yet. Waiting to do these tests until after feature stability is achieved in the software-development life cycle is not appropriate, because that requires extra work in identifying the point in time (i.e. the git commit) where the problem was introduced, and the same work identifying the correct way to manage the situation. This is much better done while the change is fresh in developers' minds, so long as the testing procedure is reasonably automatic. Also, in the gap between commit and testing, a regression may be masked by some other improvement. More extensive human-based testing before releases should still be done; but avoiding protracted bug hunts just before releases makes for a much happier team.

Cross-platform software requires extensive configuration before it can be built. The system administrator or end user needs to be able to guide what kind of GROMACS build takes place, and the configuration system needs to verify that the compiler and machine can satisfy that request. This requires searching for ways to resolve dependencies, and disclosing to the user what is being done

---

[5] http://jenkins.gromacs.org.

with what is available. It is important that compilation should not fail when configuration succeeded, because the end user is generally incapable of diagnosing what the problem was. A biochemist attempting to install GROMACS on their laptop generally does not know that scrolling back through 100 lines of output from recursive make calls is needed to find the original compilation error, and even then they will generally need to ask someone else what the problem is and how to resolve it. It is far more efficient for both users and developers to detect during configuration that compilation will fail, and to provide suggested solutions and guidance at that time. Accordingly, GROMACS uses the CMake build system (http://www.cmake.org), primarily for its cross-platform support, but makes extensive use of its high-level constructs, including sub-projects and scoped variables.

3.3   Profiling

Experience has shown that it is hard to optimize software, especially an HPC code, based on simple measurements of total execution speed. It is often necessary to have a more fine-grained view of the performance of individual parts of the code, details of execution on the individual compute units, as well as communication patterns. There is no value in measuring the improvement in execution time of a non-bonded kernel if the execution time of the FFTs is dominant!

Standard practice is to use a profiling/tracing tool to explore which functions or code lines consume important quantities of time, and to focus effort on those. However, if the measurement is to provide useful information, the profiler should perturb the execution time by a very small amount. This is particularly challenging with GROMACS because in our case an MD iteration is typically in the range of a millisecond or less wall clock time around the current scaling limit, and the functions that are interesting to profile might execute only for microseconds. Overhead introduced by performance measurement that is acceptable in other kinds of applications often leads to incorrect conclusions for GROMACS. Statistical sampling from periodically interrupting the execution to observe which core is doing which task could work in principle, but (for example) Intel's VTune 3 Amplifier defaults to a 10 ms interval, which does not create confidence that use of the tool would lead to accurate observations of events whose duration is a thousand times shorter. Reducing the profiling overhead to an acceptable level while still capturing enough information to be able to easily interpret the performance measurements has proved challenging. Additionally, this often required expert knowledge, assistance of the developers of the respective performance measurement tool. This makes it exceptionally hard to use in-depth or large-scale profiling as part of the regular GROMACS development workflow.

However, we have not been optimizing in the dark; the main mdrun simulation tool has included a built-in tracing-like functionality for many years. This functionality relies on manual instrumentation of the entire source code-base (through inlined start/stop timing functions) as well as low-overhead timing measurements based on processor cycle counters. The great benefit is that the log output of every GROMACS simulation contains a breakdown of detailed timing measurements of the different code parts. However, this internal tracing functionality does not reach its full potential because the collected data is typically displayed and analyzed through time-averages across MPI ranks and time-steps, often hiding useful details.

To realize more of this potential, we have explored the possibility of more detailed MPI rank-based statistics, including minimum and maximum execution times across ranks as well as averages. However, this information is still less detailed than that from a classical trace and profile visualizer. We are exploring combining our internal instrumentation with a tracing library. By adding API calls to various tracing libraries to our instrumentation calls, we can provide native support for detailed trace-generation in GROMACS just by linking against a tracing library like Extrae[6]. This will make it considerably easier to carry out performance analysis without the need for expert knowledge on collecting performance data while avoiding influencing the program behavior by overhead.

4   Future Directions

GROMACS has grown from an in-house simulation code into a large international software project, which now also has highly professional developer, testing and profiling environments to match it. We believe the code is quite unique in the extent to which it interacts with the underlying hardware, and while there are many significant challenges remaining this provides a very strong base for further extreme-scale computing development. However, scientific software is rapidly becoming very dependent on deep technical computing expertise: Many amazingly smart algorithms are becoming irrelevant since they cannot be implemented efficiently on modern hardware, and the inherent complexity of this hardware makes it very difficult even for highly skilled physicists and chemists to predict what will work. It is similarly not realistic to expect every research group to afford a resident computer expert, which will likely require both research groups and computing centers to increasingly join efforts to create large open source community codes where it is realistic to fund multiple full time developers. In closing, the high performance and extreme-scale computing landscape is currently changing faster than it has ever done before. It is a formidable challenge for software to keep up with this pace, but the potential rewards of exascale computing are equally large.

Acknowledgments. This work was supported by the European research Council (258980, BH), the Swedish e-Science research center, and the EU FP7 CRESTA project (287703). Computational resources were provided by the Swedish National Infrastructure for computing (grants SNIC 025/12-32 & 2013-26/24) and the Leibniz Supercomputing Center.

---

[6] http://www.bsc.es/computer-sciences/extrae.

References

1. Intel Thread Building Blocks. https://www.threadingbuildingblocks.org
2. Abraham, M.J., Gready, J.E.: Optimization of parameters for molecular dynamics simulation using smooth particle-mesh Ewald in GROMACS 4.5. J. Comput. Chem. **32**(9), 2031–2040 (2011)
3. Amdahl, G.M.: Validity of the single processor approach to achieving large scale computing capabilities. In: Proceedings of the Spring Joint Computer Conference, AFIPS 1967 (Spring), pp. 483–485. ACM, New York, NY, USA (1967). http://doi.acm.org/10.1145/1465482.1465560
4. Anderson, J.A., Lorenz, C.D., Travesset, A.: General purpose molecular dynamics simulations fully implemented on graphics processing units. J. Comput. Phys. **227**, 5324–5329 (2008)
5. Andoh, Y., Yoshii, N., Fujimoto, K., Mizutani, K., Kojima, H., Yamada, A., Okazaki, S., Kawaguchi, K., Nagao, H., Iwahashi, K., Mizutani, F., Minami, K., Ichikawa, S.I., Komatsu, H., Ishizuki, S., Takeda, Y., Fukushima, M.: MODYLAS: a highly parallelized general-purpose molecular dynamics simulation program for large-scale systems with long-range forces calculated by Fast Multipole Method (FMM) and highly scalable fine-grained new parallel processing algorithms. J. Chem. Theory Comput. **9**(7), 3201–3209 (2013). http://pubs.acs.org/doi/abs/10.1021/ct400203a
6. Arnold, A., Fahrenberger, F., Holm, C., Lenz, O., Bolten, M., Dachsel, H., Halver, R., Kabadshow, I., Gähler, F., Heber, F., Iseringhausen, J., Hofmann, M., Pippig, M., Potts, D., Sutmann, G.: Comparison of scalable fast methods for long-range interactions. Phys. Rev. E **88**, 063308 (2013). http://link.aps.org/doi/10.1103/PhysRevE.88.063308
7. Bowers, K.J., Dror, R.O., Shaw, D.E.: Overview of neutral territory methods for the parallel evaluation of pairwise particle interactions. J. Phys. Conf. Ser. **16**(1), 300 (2005). http://stacks.iop.org/1742-6596/16/i=1/a=041
8. Bowers, K.J., Dror, R.O., Shaw, D.E.: Zonal methods for the parallel execution of range-limited n-body simulations. J. Comput. Phys. **221**(1), 303–329 (2007). http://dx.doi.org/10.1016/j.jcp.2006.06.014
9. Brown, W.M., Wang, P., Plimpton, S.J., Tharrington, A.N.: Implementing molecular dynamics on hybrid high performance computers - short range forces. Comp. Phys. Comm. **182**, 898–911 (2011)
10. Eastman, P., Pande, V.S.: Efficient nonbonded interactions for molecular dynamics on a graphics processing unit. J. Comput. Chem. **31**, 1268–1272 (2010)
11. Eleftheriou, M., Moreira, J.E., Fitch, B.G., Germain, R.S.: A volumetric FFT for BlueGene/L. In: Pinkston, T.M., Prasanna, V.K. (eds.) HiPC 2003. LNCS (LNAI), vol. 2913, pp. 194–203. Springer, Heidelberg (2003)
12. Essmann, U., Perera, L., Berkowitz, M.L., Darden, T., Lee, H., Pedersen, L.G.: A smooth particle mesh Ewald method. J. Chem. Phys. **103**(19), 8577–8593 (1995)
13. Faradjian, A., Elber, R.: Computing time scales from reaction coordinates by milestoning. J. Chem. Phys. **120**, 10880–10889 (2004)
14. Hess, B., Kutzner, C., van der Spoel, D., Lindahl, E.: GROMACS 4: algorithms for highly efficient, load-balanced, and scalable molecular simulation. J. Chem. Theor. Comput. **4**(3), 435–447 (2008)
15. Humphrey, W., Dalke, A., Schulten, K.: VMD: visual molecular dynamics. J. Mol. Graph. **14**(1), 33–38 (1996)

16. Jagode, H.: Fourier transforms for the BlueGene/L communication network. Ph.D. thesis, The University of Edinburgh, Edinburgh, UK (2005)
17. Páll, S., Hess, B.: A flexible algorithm for calculating pair interactions on SIMD architectures. Comput. Phys. Commun. **184**(12), 2641–2650 (2013). http://www.sciencedirect.com/science/article/pii/S0010465513001975
18. Phillips, J.C., Braun, R., Wang, W., Gumbart, J., Tajkhorshid, E., Villa, E., Chipot, C., Skeel, R.D., Kale, L., Schulten, K.: Scalable molecular dynamics with NAMD. J. Comput. Chem. **26**, 1781–1802 (2005)
19. Pronk, S., Larsson, P., Pouya, I., Bowman, G.R., Haque, I.S., Beauchamp, K., Hess, B., Pande, V.S., Kasson, P.M., Lindahl, E.: Copernicus: A new paradigm for parallel adaptive molecular dynamics. In: Proceedings of 2011 International Conference for High Performance Computing, Networking, Storage and Analysis, SC 2011, pp. 60:1–60:10. ACM, New York, NY, USA (2011) http://doi.acm.org/10.1145/2063384.2063465
20. Pronk, S., Páll, S., Schulz, R., Larsson, P., Bjelkmar, P., Apostolov, R., Shirts, M.R., Smith, J.C., Kasson, P.M., van der Spoel, D., Hess, B., Lindahl, E.: GROMACS 4.5: a high-throughput and highly parallel open source molecular simulation toolkit. Bioinformatics **29**(7), 845–854 (2013). http://bioinformatics.oxfordjournals.org/content/29/7/845.abstract
21. Reyes, R., Turner, A., Hess, B.: Introducing SHMEM into the GROMACS molecular dynamics application: experience and results. In: Weiland, M., Jackson, A., Johnson, N. (eds.) Proceedings of the 7th International Conference on PGAS Programming Models. The University of Edinburgh, October 2013. http://www.pgas2013.org.uk/sites/default/files/pgas2013proceedings.pdf
22. Schütte, C., Winkelmann, S., Hartmann, C.: Optimal control of molecular dynamics using Markov state models. Math. Program. (Series B) **134**, 259–282 (2012)
23. Shirts, M., Pande, V.S.: Screen savers of the world unite!. Science **290**(5498), 1903–1904 (2000). http://www.sciencemag.org/content/290/5498/1903.short
24. Sugita, Y., Okamoto, Y.: Replica-exchange molecular dynamics method for protein folding. Chem. Phys. Lett. **314**, 141–151 (1999)
25. Verlet, L.: Computer "Experiments" on classical fluids. I. Thermodynamical properties of Lennard-Jones molecules. Phys. Rev. **159**, 98–103 (1967). http://link.aps.org/doi/10.1103/PhysRev.159.98
26. Wilson, G., Aruliah, D.A., Brown, C.T., Chue Hong, N.P., Davis, M., Guy, R.T., Haddock, S.H.D., Huff, K.D., Mitchell, I.M., Plumbley, M.D., Waugh, B., White, E.P., Wilson, P.: Best practices for scientific computing. PLoS Biol **12**(1), e1001745 (2014). http://dx.doi.org/10.1371/journal.pbio.1001745
27. Yokota, R., Barba, L.A.: A tuned and scalable fast multipole method as a preeminent algorithm for exascale systems. Int. J. High Perform. Comput. Appl. **26**(4), 337–346 (2012). http://hpc.sagepub.com/content/26/4/337.abstract

Weighted Decomposition in High-Performance Lattice-Boltzmann Simulations: Are Some Lattice Sites More Equal than Others?

Derek Groen[1]([⊠]), David Abou Chacra[1], Rupert W. Nash[1], Jiri Jaros[2], Miguel O. Bernabeu[1], and Peter V. Coveney[1]

[1] Centre for Computational Science, University College London,
20 Gordon Street, London WC1H 0AJ, UK
d.groen@ucl.ac.uk
[2] Faculty of Information Technology, Brno University of Technology,
Bozetechova 2, 612 66 Brno, Czech Republic
p.v.coveney@ucl.ac.uk

Abstract. Obtaining a good load balance is a significant challenge in scaling up lattice-Boltzmann simulations of realistic sparse problems to the exascale. Here we analyze the effect of weighted decomposition on the performance of the HemeLB lattice-Boltzmann simulation environment, when applied to sparse domains. Prior to domain decomposition, we assign wall and in/outlet sites with increased weights which reflect their increased computational cost. We combine our weighted decomposition with a second optimization, which is to sort the lattice sites according to a space filling curve. We tested these strategies on a sparse bifurcation and very sparse aneurysm geometry, and find that using weights reduces calculation load imbalance by up to 85 %, although the overall communication overhead is higher than some of our runs.

Keywords: High performance computing · Lattice-Boltzmann · Domain decomposition

1 Introduction

The lattice-Boltzmann (LB) method is widely applied to model fluid flow, and relies on a stream-collision scheme applied between neighbouring points on a lattice. These local interactions allow LB implementations to be efficiently parallelized, and indeed numerous high performance LB codes exist today [10,14].

Today's parallel LB implementations are able to efficiently resolve large non-sparse bulk flow systems (e.g., cuboids of fluid cells) using Petaflop supercomputers [10,12]. Efficiently modelling sparse systems on large core counts is still an unsolved problem, primarily because it is difficult to obtain a good load balance in calculation volume, neighbour count *and* communication volume for sparse geometries on large core counts [13]. Additionally, the presence of wall sites, inlets and outlets create a heterogeneity in the computational cost of different

© Springer International Publishing Switzerland 2015
S. Markidis and E. Laure (Eds.): EASC 2014, LNCS 8759, pp. 28–38, 2015.
DOI: 10.1007/978-3-319-15976-8_2

lattice sites. Here we test two techniques for their potential to improve the load balance in simulations using sparse geometries, and their performance in general.

We perform this analysis building forth on existing advances. Indeed, several LB codes already provide special decomposition techniques to more efficiently model flow in sparse geometries. For example, Palabos [1], MUSUBI [14] and WaLBerla [10] apply a block-wise decomposition strategy, while codes such as HemeLB [13] and MUPHY [19] rely on third-party partitioning libraries such as ParMETIS and PT_Scotch.

Here we implement and test a weighted decomposition technique to try and improve the parallel simulation performance of the HemeLB simulation environment for sparse geometries [16], by adding weights corresponding to the computational cost of lattice sites which do not represent bulk fluid sites. In addition, we examine the effect of also pre-ordering the lattice via a space-filling curve when applying this method.

Several other groups have investigated the use of weighted decomposition in other areas, for example in environmental fluid mechanics [5]. In addition, Catalyurek et al. [9] investigate adaptive repartitioning with Zoltan using weighted graphs. Specifically, Axner et al. [4] applied a weighting technique to a lattice-Boltzmann solver for sparse geometries. Whereas we apply weights to vertices, they applied heavier weights to edges near in- and outlets, to ensure that these regions would not be distributed across several processes.

2   HemeLB

HemeLB is a high performance parallel lattice-Boltzmann code for large scale fluid flow in complex geometries. It is mainly written in C++. HemeLB supports a range of boundary conditions and collision operators [18] and features a streaming visualization and steering client [13,17]. In addition, we have equipped HemeLB with a coupling interface, allowing it to be used as part of a multiscale simulation [11]. HemeLB uses the coalesced communication design pattern to manage its communications [8], and relies on non-blocking point-to-point MPI send and receive calls to perform data movements during the simulation. We present the improvement in performance of HemeLB over time in Fig. 1. We obtained the performance data for this figure from a variety of sources (e.g., [13,16,17]). Overall, the peak performance of HemeLB has improved by more than a factor 25 between 2007 and 2014, although we do now distinguish some difference in peak performance between simulations with sparse geometries (e.g., aneurysm models) and those with non-sparse geometries (e.g., cylinders). Most recently, we obtained a performance of 153 MSUPS using 49,152 cores on the ARCHER supercomputer [2]. The geometry used in these runs was a cylinder containing 230 million lattice sites.

HemeLB originally performs decomposition in two stages, making use of the ParMETIS graph partitioning library [3] version 4.0.2. In the first stage it loads the lattice arranged as blocks of 8 by 8 by 8 lattice sites. These blocks are distributed across the processes, favoring adjacent blocks when a process receives

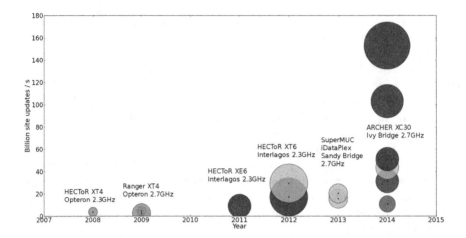

Fig. 1. Overview of the obtained calculation performance (in billions of lattice site updates per second as a function of the years in which the simulation runs were performed. The runs were performed on a variety of supercomputers, each of which is briefly described above or below the respective data points. The number of cores used is shown by the size of the circle, ranging from 2,048 cores (smallest circles) to 49,152 cores (largest circles). The fluid fraction is shown by the color of the circle. These include very sparse simulation domains such as vascular networks (red circles), sparse domains such as bifurcations (green circles), ranging to non-sparse domains such cylinders (blue circles) (Color figure online).

multiple blocks [16]. After this initial decomposition, HemeLB then uses the `ParMETIS_V3_PartKWay()` function to optimize the decomposition, abandoning the original block-level structure [13]. This function relies on a K-way partitioning technique, which first shrinks the geometry to a minimally decomposable size, then performs the decomposition, and then refines the geometry back to its original size. One of the ways we can assess the quality of the decomposition is by examining the *edge cut*, which is equal to the number of lattice neighbour links that cross process boundaries.

3 Description of the Optimizations

We have implemented and tested two optimizations in the decomposition.

3.1 Weighting

Within sparse geometries, lattice-Boltzmann codes generally adopt a range of lattice site types to encapsulate all the functionalities required to treat flow in bulk, near walls and near in- and outlets. We provide a simple example of a geometry containing these lattice site types in Fig. 2. By default, all types of lattice sites are weighted equally in HemeLB, which means that graph partitioners such as ParMETIS treat all site types with equal importance when creating a

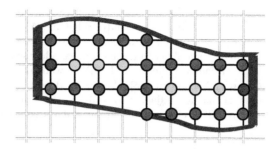

Fig. 2. 2D example of a sparse domain with the different types of lattice sites. In/outlets are given by the blue bars and vessel walls by the red curves. Bulk sites are shown by yellow dots, wall sites by green dots, wall in/outlet sites by red dots, and in/outlet sites by blue dots (Color figure online).

domain decomposition. However, we find that both sites adjacent to walls and sites adjacent to in- and outlets require more computational time to be updated. To optimize the load balance of the code, we therefore assign heavier weights to sites which reside adjacent to wall or in/outlet boundaries.

We are currently developing an automated tuning implementation to obtain these computational costs at run-time. However, as a first proof of concept, we have deduced approximate weighting values by running six simulations of cylinders with different aspect ratios. The shorter and wider cylinders have a relatively high ratio of in- and outlet sites, while the longer and more narrow cylinders have a relatively high ratio of wall sites. In addition, the cylinders with an aspect ratio near 1:1 have a relatively high ratio of bulk flow sites.

Based on these runs we have obtained estimated values for the computational cost for each type of lattice site, by using a least-square fitting function. We present the values of these fits, as well as rounded values we use in ParMETIS, in Table 1. ParMETIS supports using weights in graphs, provided that these weights are given as integers. As we found that using large numbers for these weights has a negative effect on the stability of ParMETIS, we chose to normalize and round the weightings such that bulk sites are given a weight of 4, and the other site types are given by values relative to that base value. Because the test runs contained only a very small number of wall + in/outlet sites, we choose to adopt the weighting for in/outlet sites also for the in/outlet sites which are adjacent to a wall boundary.

3.2   Using a Space-Filling Curve

A second, and more straightforward, optimization we have applied is by taking the Cartesian x, y and z coordinates of all lattice sites, and then sorting them according to Morton-ordered space-filling curve. We do this prior to partitioning the simulation domain, and in doing so, we effectively eliminate any bias introduced by the early stage decomposition scheme described in [16]. We do this by replacing the `ParMETIS_V3_PartKWay()` in the code function with a

Table 1. Weight values as obtained from fitting against the runtimes of six test simulations on two compute architectures (Intel SandyBridge and AMD Interlagos). The site type is given, followed by the weigh obtained from fitting the performance data of the six runs, followed by the simplified integer value we adopted in ParMETIS. In this work we use Bouzidi-Firdaouss-Lallemand (BFL) [7] wall conditions and in and outlet conditions described in Nash et al. [18]. We observed rather erratic fits for the weightings of in/outlet sites that are adjacent to walls, as these made up only a very marginal fraction of the overall site counts in our benchmark runs (less than 1 % in most cases).

Site type	Obtained weight		Rounded weight
	Intel	AMD	
Bulk	10.0	10.0	4
Wall (BFL)	18.708	20.226	8
In/outlet	40.037	37.398	16
Wall and in/outlet	22.700[a]	34.577[a]	16

[a]Only very few sites in a given geometry are both adjacent to a wall and to an in/outlet. As such, the weighting values we obtained for this site type are considerably less accurate than those for the other site types.

`ParMETIS_V3_PartGeomKWay()` function. This optimization is functionally independent from the weighted decomposition technique, but can lead to a better decomposition result from ParMETIS when applied.

3.3   Other Optimizations We Have Considered

After having inserted these optimizations, we have also tried improving the partition by reducing the tolerance in ParMETIS. The amount of load imbalance permitted within ParMETIS is indicated by the tolerance value, and a lower value will increase the number of iterations ParMETIS will do to reach its final state. Decreasing the tolerance from 1.001 to 1.00001 resulted for us in an increase of the ParMETIS processing time while showing a negligible difference in the quality of partitioning. As a result, we have chosen not to investigate this optimization in this work.

4   Setup

In our performance tests we used two different simulation domains. These include a smaller *bifurcation* geometry and a larger *aneurysm* geometry (see Fig. 3 for both). The bifurcation simulation domain consists of 650492 lattice sites, which occupy about 10 % of the bounding box of the geometry. The aneurysm simulation domain consists of 5667778 lattice sites, which occupy about 1.5 % of the bounding box of the geometry. We run our simulations using pressure in- and outlets described in Nash et al. [18], the LBGK collision operator [6], the D3Q19 advection model and Bouzidi-Firdaouss-Lallemand wall conditions [7].

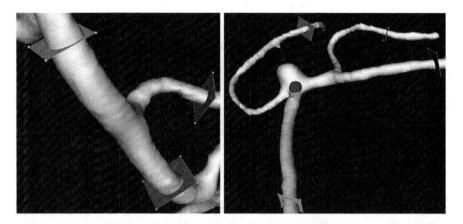

Fig. 3. Overview of the bifurcation geometry (left) and the aneurysm geometry (right) used in our performance tests. The blue blob in the aneurysm geometry is a marker indicating a region of specific interest to the user. The bifurcation geometry has a sparsity of about 10 % (i.e., the lattice sites occupy about 10 % of the bounding box of the geometry), and the aneurysm geometry a sparsity of about 1.5 % (Color figure online).

For our benchmarks we use the HECToR Cray XT6 supercomputer at EPCC in Edinburgh, and compile our code using the GCC compiler version 4.3.4. We have run our simulations for 50000 time steps using 128–1024 cores for the bifurcation simulation domain, and 512–12288 cores for the aneurysm simulation domain. We repeated the run for each core count five times and averaged the results. We do this because the scheduler at HECToR does not necessarily allocate processes within a single job to adjacent nodes; and as a result the performance differs between runs. We have also performed several runs using the aneurysm simulation domain on the ARCHER Cray XC30 supercomputer at EPCC. These runs were performed with an otherwise identical configuration. ARCHER relies on an Intel Ivy Bridge architecture and has a peak performance of about 1.6 PFLOPs in total.

5   Results

We present our measurements of the total simulation time and the maximum LB calculation time for the bifurcation simulation domain in Fig. 4.

We find that both incorporating a space-filling curve and using weighted decomposition results in a reduction of the simulation time. However, the use of a space-filling curve does little to reduce the calculation load imbalance, whereas enabling weighted decomposition results in a reduction of the calculation load imbalance by up to 85 %. We also examined the edge-cut returned by ParMETIS during the domain decomposition stage. For each core count, the edge cut obtained in all the runs was within a margin of 4.5 %, with slightly higher edge cuts for runs using a space-filling curve or weighted decomposition.

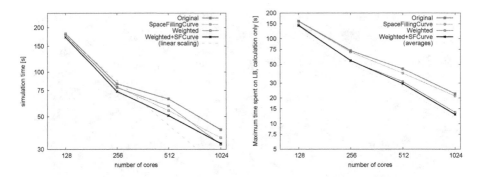

Fig. 4. Total simulation time and maximum LB calculation time for the simulation using the bifurcation model, run on HECToR. We performed measurements for the non-optimized code, a code with only weighting enabled, a code with only the space-filling curve enabled, and a code with both enabled. We provide lines to guide the eyes. In the image on the left we plotted a linear scaling line using a thick gray dotted line. In the image on the right we plotted the average LB calculation time of all our run types using thin gray dotted lines (Color figure online).

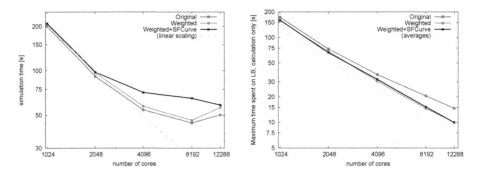

Fig. 5. Total simulation time and maximum LB calculation time for the simulation of the aneurysm model, run on HECToR. See Fig. 4 for an explanation of the lines and symbols. Here we only performed measurements for the non-optimized code, a code with only the space-filling curve optimization enabled, and a code with both optimizations enabled.

We present our measurements of the total simulation time and the maximum LB calculation time for the aneurysm simulation domain in Fig. 5. Here we find that applying weighted decomposition results in an increase of runtime by ∼5 % in most of our runs. Using the space-filling curve in addition to the weighted decomposition results in a further increase in runtime, especially for runs performed on 4096 and 8192 cores. However, the use of weighted decomposition also results in a calculation load imbalance which is up to 65 % lower than that of the original simulation, while we again observe little difference here between runs that use a space-filling curve and the runs without. When we examine the edge

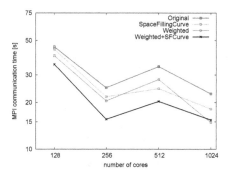
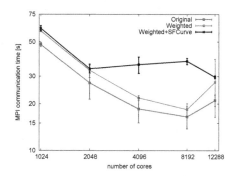

Fig. 6. Total MPI communication time for the simulation of the bifurcation model (left, from the run presented in Fig. 4) and the aneurysm model (right, from the run presented in Fig. 5).

cut obtained by ParMETIS in different runs, we find that using weighted decomposition results in a slightly lower edge cut ($\sim$0.5 %) and using a space-filling curve results in an edge cut which is up to 5.3 % higher.

To provide more insight into the cause of the increase in simulation time, we present our measurements of the MPI communication overhead in these runs in Fig. 6. Here the runs which use our optimization strategies take less time to do MPI communication when applied to the bifurcation simulation domain, and more time to do MPI communications when applied to the aneurysm domain. These differences match largely with the differences we observed in the overall simulation time. Because the total time spent on MPI communications is generally larger than the calculation time for high core counts, and the differences between the runs are considerable, the communication performance is a major component of the overall simulation performance. However, the communication performance correlates only weakly with the edge cut values returned by ParMETIS and therefore the total communication volume. For example, the slightly lower edge cut for the aneurysm simulations with weighted decomposition is in contrast with the slightly higher communication overhead. This means that the *communication load imbalance* is likely to be a major bottleneck in the performance of our larger runs, and should be investigated more closely.

5.1   Performance Results on ARCHER

We have repeated the simulations using the aneurysm simulation domain on the ARCHER supercomputer, both with and without using weighted decomposition. We present the measured simulation and calculation times of these runs in Fig. 7, and the MPI communication time in Fig. 8. In these runs, we obtained approximately three times the performance per core compared to HECToR. When using weighted decomposition, the calculation load imbalance was reduced by up to 70 %, the simulation time by approximately 2–12 % and the MPI communication time by approximately 5–20 %. In particular, the reduction in communication

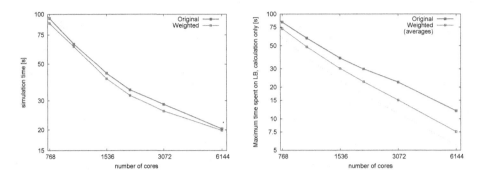

Fig. 7. Total simulation time and maximum LB calculation time for the simulation of the aneurysm model, as run on ARCHER. See Fig. 4 for an explanation of the lines and symbols. Here we only performed measurements for the non-optimized code, and a code with weighted decomposition enabled.

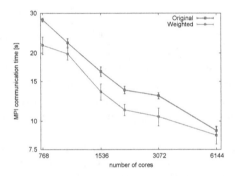

Fig. 8. Total MPI communication time for the run presented in Fig. 7.

time contrasts with the measured increase in communication time, which we observed in the HECToR runs. This difference could be attributed to the superior network architecture of ARCHER, and/or the large memory per core, which may have resulted in ParMETIS reaching a domain decomposition with better communication load balance.

6   Discussion and Conclusions

We presented an approach for weighted decomposition and assessed its effect on the performance of the HemeLB bloodflow simulation environment. The use of lattice weights in our decomposition scheme provides the strongest improvement in calculation load balance, and delivers an improvement in the simulation performance for the bifurcation geometry. However, the use of weighted decomposition (both with and without the space-filling curve optimization) sometimes results in a higher communication overhead of the aneurysm simulations, despite negligible changes in the communication volume. Indeed, for these blood flow simulations it appears that a low edge cut is only a minor factor in the overall communication performance for sparse problems, even though graph partitioning libraries are frequently optimized to accomplish such a minimal edge cut. This is in accordance with some earlier conclusions in the literature [15]. We intend to more thoroughly investigate the communication load imbalance of our larger runs. As part of preparing HemeLB for the exascale within the CRESTA project, we are working with experts from the Deutschen Zentrums für Lucht und Raumfahrt (DLR) to enable domain decompositions using PT-Scotch and Zoltan. The use of these alternate graph partitioning libraries may result in further performance improvements, especially if these libraries optimize not only for a calculation load balance and a low edge cut, but also take into account other communication characteristics. Furthermore, since we have observed differences in site weights between different computer architectures, we are looking into an "auto-tuning" function that automatically calculates the weights at runtime or compilation time.

Acknowledgements. We thank Timm Krueger for his valuable input. This work has received funding from the CRESTA and MAPPER projects within the EC-FP7 (ICT-2011.9.13) under Grant Agreements nos. 287703 and 261507, and from EPSRC Grants EP/I017909/1 (www.2020science.net) and EP/I034602/1. This work made use of the HECToR supercomputer at EPCC in Edinburgh, funded by the Office of Science and Technology through EPSRC's High End Computing Programme.

References

1. Palabos LBM Wiki (2011). http://wiki.palabos.org/
2. Cresta case study: application soars above petascale after tools collaboration (2014). http://www.cresta-project.eu/images/cresta_casestudy1_2014.pdf
3. ParMETIS (2014). http://glaros.dtc.umn.edu/gkhome/metis/parmetis/overview
4. Axner, L., Bernsdorf, J., Zeiser, T., Lammers, P., Linxweiler, J., Hoekstra, A.G.: Performance evaluation of a parallel sparse lattice Boltzmann solver. J. Computat. Phys. **227**(10), 4895–4911 (2008)
5. Barad, M.F., Colella, P., Schladow, S.G.: An adaptive cut-cell method for environmental fluid mechanics. Int. J. Numer. Methods Fluids **60**(5), 473–514 (2009)
6. Bhatnagar, P.L., Gross, E.P., Krook, M.: A model for collision processes in gases. i. small amplitude processes in charged and neutral one-component systems. Phys. Rev. **94**, 511–525 (1954)
7. Bouzidi, M., Firdaouss, M., Lallemand, P.: Momentum transfer of a Boltzmann-lattice fluid with boundaries. Phys. Fluids **13**(11), 3452–3459 (2001)
8. Carver, H.B., Groen, D., Hetherington, J., Nash, R.W., Bernabeu, M.O., Coveney, P.V.: Coalesced communication: a design pattern for complex parallel scientific software. Advances in Engineering Software (2015, in press)
9. Catalyurek, U.V., Boman, E.G., Devine, K.D., Bozdag, D., Heaphy, R., Riesen, L.A.: Hypergraph-based dynamic load balancing for adaptive scientific computations. In: IEEE International Parallel and Distributed Processing Symposium, 2007, IPDPS 2007, pp. 1–11. IEEE (2007)

10. Godenschwager, C., Schornbaum, F., Bauer, M., Köstler, H., Rüde, U.: A framework for hybrid parallel flow simulations with a trillion cells in complex geometries. In: Proceedings of SC13: International Conference for High Performance Computing, Networking, Storage and Analysis, SC 2013, pp. 35:1–35:12. ACM, New York (2013)

11. Groen, D., Borgdorff, J., Bona-Casas, C., Hetherington, J., Nash, R.W., Zasada, S.J., Saverchenko, I., Mamonski, M., Kurowski, K., Bernabeu, M.O., Hoekstra, A.G., Coveney, P.V.: Flexible composition and execution of high performance, high fidelity multiscale biomedical simulations. Interface Focus **3**(2), 20120087 (2013)

12. Groen, D., Henrich, O., Janoschek, F., Coveney, P.V., Harting, J.: Lattice-boltzmann methods in fluid dynamics: turbulence and complex colloidal fluids. In: Jülich Blue Gene/P Extreme Scaling Workshop (2011)

13. Groen, D., Hetherington, J., Carver, H.B., Nash, R.W., Bernabeu, M.O., Coveney, P.V.: Analyzing and modeling the performance of the HemeLB lattice-Boltzmann simulation environment. J. Comput. Sci. **4**(5), 412–422 (2013)

14. Hasert, M., Masilamani, K., Zimny, S., Klimach, H., Qi, J., Bernsdorf, J., Roller, S.: Complex fluid simulations with the parallel tree-based lattice boltzmannsolver musubi. J. Comput. Sci. **5**, 784–794 (2013)

15. Hendrickson, B., Kolda, T.G.: Graph partitioning models for parallel computing. Parallel Comput. **26**(12), 1519–1534 (2000)

16. Mazzeo, M.D., Coveney, P.V.: HemeLB: a high performance parallel lattice-Boltzmann code for large scale fluid flow in complex geometries. Comput. Phys. Commun. **178**(12), 894–914 (2008)

17. Mazzeo, M.D., Manos, S., Coveney, P.V.: In situ ray tracing and computational steering for interactive blood flow simulation. Comput. Phys. Commun. **181**, 355–370 (2010)

18. Nash, R.W., Carver, H.B., Bernabeu, M.O., Hetherington, J., Groen, D., Krüger, T., Coveney, P.V.: Choice of boundary condition for lattice-Boltzmann simulation of moderate Reynolds number flow in complex domains. Phys. Rev. E **89**, 023303 (2014)

19. Peters, A., Melchionna, S., Kaxiras, E., Lätt, J., Sircar, J., Bernaschi, M., Bison, M., Succi, S.: Multiscale simulation of cardiovascular flows on the ibm bluegene/p: full heart-circulation system at red-blood cell resolution. In: Proceedings of the 2010 ACM/IEEE International Conference for High Performance Computing, Networking, Storage and Analysis, SC 2010, Washington, DC, USA, pp. 1–10. IEEE Computer Society (2010)

Performance Analysis of a Reduced Data Movement Algorithm for Neutron Cross Section Data in Monte Carlo Simulations

John R. Tramm[1]($\boxtimes$), Andrew R. Siegel[1], Benoit Forget[2], and Colin Josey[2]

[1] Center for Exascale Simulation for Advanced Reactors,
Argonne National Laboratory, Lemont, USA
jtramm@mcs.anl.gov
[2] Department of Nuclear Science and Engineering,
Massachusetts Institute of Technology, Cambridge, USA

Abstract. Current Monte Carlo neutron transport applications use continuous energy cross section data to provide the statistical foundation for particle trajectories. This "classical" algorithm requires storage and random access of very large data structures. Recently, Forget et al. [1] reported on a fundamentally new approach, based on multipole expansions, that distills cross section data down to a more abstract mathematical format. Their formulation greatly reduces memory storage and improves data locality at the cost of also increasing floating point computation. In the present study, we abstract the multipole representation into a "proxy application", which we then use to determine the hardware performance parameters of the algorithm relative to the classical continuous energy algorithm. This study is done to determine the viability of both algorithms on current and next-generation high performance computing platforms.

Keywords: Monte carlo · Multi-core · Neutron transport · Reactor simulation · Multipole · Cross section

1 Introduction

Monte Carlo (MC) transport algorithms are considered the "gold standard" of accuracy for a broad range of applications – e.g., nuclear reactor physics, shielding, detection, medical dosimetry, and weapons design to name just a few examples. In the design and analysis of nuclear reactor cores, the key application driver of the present analysis, MC methods for neutron transport offer significant potential advantages compared to deterministic methods given their simplicity, avoidance of ad hoc approximations in energy treatment, and lack of need for complex computational meshing of reactor geometries.

On the other hand it is well known that robust analysis of a full reactor core is still beyond the reach of MC methods. Tremendous advances have been made in recent years, but the computing requirements for full quasi-static depletion

© Springer International Publishing Switzerland 2015
S. Markidis and E. Laure (Eds.): EASC 2014, LNCS 8759, pp. 39–56, 2015.
DOI: 10.1007/978-3-319-15976-8_3

analysis of commercial reactor cores is a performance-bound problem, even on existing leadership class computers. It is also clear that many of the issues related to scalability on distributed memory machines have been adequately addressed in recent studies [2,3], and that the path to future speedups involves taking better advantage of a broad range of multi-core systems. For MC methods this is most naturally done, as a first step, in a MIMD context, which allows us to most easily exploit the natural parallelism over particle tracks, each with complex, nested branching logic. Siegel et al. [4] carried out an in-depth study of on-node scalability of the *OpenMC* [2] transport code, showing encouraging results as well as limitations due to memory contention. Tramm et al. [5,6] carried out an in-depth study based on the *XSBench* mini-application, further elucidating the underlying performance bottlenecks that inhibit scalability. Indeed, with less memory bandwidth per core as nodes become more complex, developing new approaches that minimize memory contention and maximize use of each core's floating point units becomes increasingly important.

Recently, Forget et al. [1] proposed a new algorithm for representing neutron cross section data in a more memory efficient manner. This algorithm, based on multipole expansions, compresses data into a more abstract mathematical format. This greatly reduces the memory footprint of the cross section data and improves data locality at the expense of an increase in the number of computations required to reconstruct it when it is needed. As next-generation leadership class computers are likely to favor floating point operations over data movement [7–10], the multipole algorithm may provide significant performance improvement compared to the classical approach.

In this analysis we study in-depth two different implementations of the MC neutron transport algorithm – the "classical" continuous energy cross section format and the multipole representation format. Then, we assess the on-node scaling properties and memory contention issues of these algorithms in the context of a reactor physics calculation.

1.1 The Reactor Simulation Problem

Computer-based simulation of nuclear reactors is a well established field, with origins dating back to the early years of digital computing. Traditional reactor simulation techniques aim to solve deterministic equations (typically a variant of the diffusion equation) for a given material geometry and initial neutron distribution (source) within the reactor. This is done using mature and well understood numerical methods. Deterministic codes are capable of running quickly and providing relatively accurate gross power distributions, but are still limited when accurate localized effects are required, such as e.g. at sharp material interfaces.

An alternative formulation, the Monte Carlo (MC) method, simulates the path of individual neutrons as they travel through the reactor core. As many particle histories are simulated and tallied, a picture of the full distribution of neutrons within the domain emerges. Such codes are inherently simple, easy to understand, and potentially easy to restructure when porting to new systems. Furthermore, the methodologies utilized by MC simulation require very few assumptions, resulting in highly accurate results given adequate statistical convergence. The downside to this method, however, is that a huge number of neutron histories are required to achieve an acceptably low variance in the results. For many problems this means an impractically long time to solution, though such limitations may be overcome given the increased computational power of next-generation, exascale supercomputers.

1.2 OpenMC

OpenMC is a Monte Carlo particle transport simulation code focused on neutron criticality calculations [2]. It is capable of simulating 3D models based on constructive solid geometry with second-order surfaces. The particle interaction data is based on ACE format cross sections, also used in the *MCNP* and *Serpent* Monte Carlo codes.

OpenMC was originally developed by members of the Computational Reactor Physics Group at the Massachusetts Institute of Technology starting in 2011. Various universities, laboratories, and other organizations now contribute to its development. The application is written in FORTRAN, with parallelism supported by a hybrid OpenMP/MPI model. *OpenMC* is an open source software project available online [11].

1.3 XSBench

The *XSBench* proxy application models the most computationally intensive part of a typical MC reactor core transport algorithm – the calculation of macroscopic neutron cross sections, a kernel which accounts for around 85 % of the total runtime of *OpenMC* [4]. *XSBench* retains the essential performance-related computational conditions and tasks of fully featured reactor core MC neutron transport codes, yet at a fraction of the programming complexity of the full application [6]. Particle tracking and other features of the full MC transport algorithm were not included in *XSBench* as they take up only a small portion of runtime in robust reactor computations. This provides a much simpler and far more transparent platform for testing the algorithm on different architectures, making alterations to the code, and collecting hardware runtime performance data.

XSBench was developed by members of the Center for Exascale Simulation of Advanced Reactors (CESAR) at Argonne National Laboratory. The application is written in C, with multi-core parallelism support provided by OpenMP. *XSBench* is an open source software project. All source code is publicly available online [12].

1.4 RSBench

The *RSBench* proxy application is similar in purpose to *XSBench*, but models an alternative method for calculating neutron cross sections – the multipole method. This method organizes the data into a significantly more compact form, saving several orders of magnitude in memory space. However, this method also requires "unpacking" of this data by way of a significant number of additional computations (FLOPs). The multipole algorithm has also been experimentally implemented into *OpenMC*, but is only capable of simulating several select nuclides with this method due to limited multipole cross section library support.

RSBench is in active development by members of the CESAR group at Argonne National Laboratory. The application is written in C, with multi-core parallelism support provided by OpenMP. *RSBench* is an open source software project. All source code is publicly available online [13].

2   Algorithm

2.1   Reactor Model

When carrying out reactor core analysis, the geometry and material properties of a postulated nuclear reactor must be specified in order to define the variables and scope of the simulation model. For the purposes of *XSBench* and *RSBench*, we use a well known community reactor benchmark known as the Hoogenboom-Martin model [14]. This model is a simplified analog to a more complete, "real-world" reactor problem, and provides a standardized basis for discussions on performance within the reactor simulation community. *XSBench* and *RSBench* recreate the computational conditions present when fully featured MC neutron transport codes (such as *OpenMC*) simulate the Hoogenboom-Martin reactor model, preserving a similar data structure, a similar level of randomness of data accesses, and a similar distribution of FLOPs and memory loads.

2.2   Neutron Cross Sections

The purpose of an MC particle transport reactor simulation is to calculate the distribution and generation rates of neutrons within a nuclear reactor. In order to achieve this goal, a large number of neutron lifetimes are simulated by tracking the path and interactions of a neutron through the reactor from its birth in a fission event to its escape or absorption, the latter possibly resulting in subsequent fission events.

Each neutron in the simulation is described by three primary factors: its spatial location within a reactor's geometry, its speed, and its direction. At each stage of the transport calculation, a determination must be made as to what the particle will do next. Possible outcomes include uninterrupted continuation of free flight, collision, or absorption (possibly resulting in fission). The determination of which event occurs is based on a random sampling of a statistical distribution that is described by empirical material data stored in main memory. This data, called *neutron cross section data*, represents the probability that a neutron of a particular speed (energy) will undergo some particular interaction when it is inside a given type of material.

To account for neutrons across a wide energy spectrum and materials of many different types, the classical algorithm, as represented by *XSBench*, requires use of a very large data structure that holds cross section data points for many discrete energy levels. In the case of the simplified Hoogenboom-Martin benchmark, roughly 5.6 GB[1] of data is required. The multipole method greatly reduces these requirements down the the order of approximately 100 MB or less for all data.

2.3   Classical Continuous Energy Cross Section Representation

The classical continuous energy cross section representation, as used by real world applications like *OpenMC*, is abstracted in the proxy-application *XSBench*. This section describes the data structure used by this algorithm along with the access patterns of the algorithm.

Data Structure. A material in the Hoogenboom-Martin reactor model is composed of a mixture of nuclides. For instance, the "reactor fuel" material might consist of several hundred different nuclides, while the "pressure vessel side wall" material might only contain a dozen or so. In total, there are 12 different materials and 355 different nuclides present in the modeled reactor. The data usage requirements to store this model are significant, totaling 5.6 GB, as summarized in Table 1.

Table 1. *XSBench* data structure summary

Nuclides tracked	355
Total # of energy gridpoints	4,012,565
Cross section interaction types	5
Total size of cross section data structures	5.6 GB

For each nuclide, an array of nuclide grid points are stored as data in main memory. Each nuclide grid point (as represented in Fig. 1) has an energy level, as well as five cross section values (corresponding to five different particle interaction types) for that energy level. The grid points are ordered from lowest to highest energy levels. The number, distribution, and granularity of energy levels varies between nuclides. One nuclide may have hundreds of thousands of grid points clustered around lower energy levels, while another nuclide may only have a few hundred grid points distributed across the full energy spectrum. This obviates straightforward approaches to uniformly organizing and accessing the data. Collectively, this data structure (depicted in Fig. 2) is known as the *nuclide energy grid*.

In order to increase the speed of the calculation, the algorithm utilizes another data structure, called the *unionized energy grid*, as described by Leppänen [16] and Romano [2]. The unionized grid facilitates fast lookups of cross section data from

---

[1] We estimate that for a robust depletion calculation, in excess of 100 GB of cross section data would be required [15].

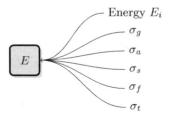

Fig. 1. A cross section data packet for a neutron within a given nuclide at a given energy level, E_i.

the nuclide grids. This structure is an array of grid points, consisting of an energy level and a set of pointers to the closest corresponding energy level on each of the different nuclide grids (Fig. 3).

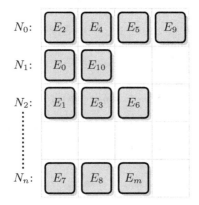

Fig. 2. Simplified example of the nuclide energy grid. Note how each nuclide has a varying number and distribution of energy levels.

Access Patterns. In a full MC neutron transport application, the data structure is accessed each time a macroscopic cross section needs to be calculated. This happens anytime a particle changes energy (via a collision) or crosses a material boundary within the reactor. These macroscopic cross section calculations occur with very high frequency in the MC transport algorithm, and the inputs to them are effectively random. For the sake of simplicity, *XSBench* was written ignoring the particle tracking aspect of the MC neutron transport algorithm and instead isolates the macroscopic cross section lookup kernel. This provides a large reduction in program complexity while retaining similarly random input conditions for the macroscopic cross section lookups via the use of a random number generator.

In *XSBench*, each macroscopic cross section lookup consists of two randomly sampled inputs: the neutron energy E_p, and the material m_p. Given these two

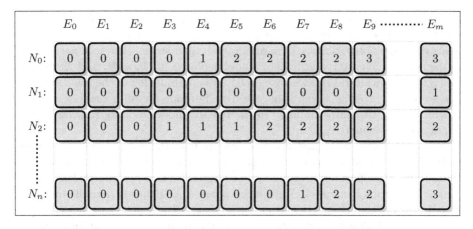

Fig. 3. Simplified example of the unionized energy grid. Each grid element is the index where the energy level E_i can be found in the nuclide energy grid for nuclide N_i.

inputs, a binary search that executes in $\log(n)$ time is done on the unionized energy grid for the given energy. Once the correct entry is found on the unionized energy grid, the material input is used to perform lookups from the nuclide grids present in the material. Use of the unionized energy grid means that binary searches are not required on each individual nuclide grid. For each nuclide present in the material, the two bounding nuclide grid points are found using the pointers from the unionized energy grid and interpolated to give the exact microscopic cross section at that point.

All calculated microscopic cross sections are then accumulated (weighted by their atomic density in the given material), which results in the macroscopic cross section for the material. Algorithm 1 is an abbreviated summary of this calculation.

Algorithm 1. Classical Continuous Energy Macroscopic Cross Section Lookup

---
1: $R(m_p, E_p)$ ▷ randomly sample inputs
2: Locate E_p on Unionized Grid   ▷ binary search
3: **for** $n \in m_p$ **do**   ▷ for each nuclide in input material
4:     $\sigma_a \leftarrow n, E_p$ ▷ lookup bounding micro xs's
5:     $\sigma_b \leftarrow n, E_p + 1$
6:     $\sigma \leftarrow \sigma_a, \sigma_b$ ▷ interpolate
7:     $\Sigma \leftarrow \Sigma + \rho_n \cdot \sigma$ ▷ accumulate macro xs
8: **end for**

In theory, one could "pre-compute" all macroscopic cross sections on the unionized energy grid for each material. This would allow the algorithm to run much faster, requiring far fewer memory loads and far fewer floating point operations per macroscopic cross section lookup. However, this would assume a static distribution of nuclides within a material. In practice, MC transport nuclide-depletion calculations are quasi-static; they will need to track the burn-up of fuels and account for heterogeneous temperature distributions within the reactor itself. This means that concentrations are dynamic, rather than static, therefore necessitating the use of the more versatile data model deployed in *OpenMC* and *XSBench*. Even if static concentrations were assumed, pre-computation of the full spectrum of macroscopic cross sections would need to be done for all geometric regions (of which there are many millions) in the reactor model, leading to even higher memory requirements.

We have verified that *XSBench* faithfully mimics the data access patterns of the full MC application under a broad range of conditions [6]. The runtime of full-scale MC transport applications, such as *OpenMC*, is 85 % composed of macroscopic cross section lookups [4]. Within this process, *XSBench* is virtually indistinguishable from *OpenMC*, as the same type and size of data structure is used, with a similarly random access pattern and a similar number of floating point operations occurring between memory loads. Thus, performance analysis done with *XSBench* provides results applicable to the full MC neutron transport algorithm, while being far easier to implement, run, and interpret.

2.4 Multipole Cross Section Representation

A multipole representation cross section algorithm is abstracted in the proxy-application *RSBench*. This section summarizes the data structure used by this algorithm along with the access patterns and computations performed by the algorithm. The multipole representation stores cross section data in the form of poles. Each pole can be characterized by several variables that define the parameters (residues) of the resonance that can be used to compute the actual microscopic cross section contribution at any energy from the pole. Forget et al. also utilize a "window" methodology that limits the number of poles that need to be evaluated for a given cross section calculation [1]. The energy spectrum is broken up into a series of windows, each covering a specific energy range and storing a set of fitting factors. These fitting factors represent a "background" function that can be evaluated to represent the contributions from all poles outside the window. Use of the windowing method saves time by requiring that only poles within a single energy window need to be evaluated to determine the microscopic cross sections, rather than all poles in the entire energy spectrum. A more in-depth explanation of the mathematics behind the multipole representation is offered by Forget et al. [1].

Data Structure. The primary data structures employed by *RSBench* are two separate 2-D jagged arrays. The first 2-D array contains the resonance data for all poles and accompanying residues. The first dimension correlates to each nuclide present in the reactor. The second dimension correlates to the number of poles present in that nuclide (each nuclide has a different number of poles, varying from 100 to 6,000) [1]. For the purposes of this mini-app, a representative average number of poles per nuclide is set at 1,000 as default. Each element of this array is a "pole" data structure that holds several pieces of information including the center energy for the pole, resonance residues for several reaction types, and the l index, as depicted in Fig. 4.

The second 2-D array contains data for all windows. The first dimension correlates to each nuclide present in in the reactor. The second dimension correlates to the number of windows used for that particular nuclide. Window sizing is an empirical process done when building a library of multipole cross section data, where each nuclide is likely to require a different window size to achieve a given accuracy. Thus, each nuclide in *RSBench* has a different number of windows (ranging from 4 to 25 poles per window [1]). For the purposes of this mini-app, a representative number of windows is set to 250 as default. Each element of this array is a window data structure that holds several pieces of information including the function fitting factors for several reaction types and the start and end pole indices, as represented in Fig. 5.

Compared to the classical method, such as used by *XSBench*, these 2-D arrays together are in total much smaller as no unionized energy grid is necessary and far fewer data points are needed, as summarized in Table 2. Use of the multipole method in this case results in a memory footprint reduction of over two orders of magnitude.

Note that the average number of poles per nuclide and windows per nuclide used in *RSBench* are only approximations. Multipole data requirements are well understood for U-235 and U-238, but library files have yet to be computed for the other 353 nuclides in our simulation. Approximations were selected based on interpolation, under the assumption that multipole memory requirements from U-235 and U-238 will have similar ratios of data memory requirements compared to the other nuclides for the classical continuous energy cross section storage method. E.g., the ratio of data storage needed between U-238 and Ni-58 for continuous energy representation will remain the same for multipole representation.

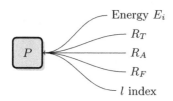

Fig. 4. Data structure representing a pole and accompanying residues, centered at E_i.

Access Patterns. The macroscopic cross section algorithm used by *RSBench* is similar to *XSBench* at a high level, only deviating at the lower level where microscopic cross sections are determined. A macroscopic cross section lookup begins with the same two randomized inputs: the neutron energy and the material the neutron is located in. From here, the nuclides that the material contains are looped over. For each nuclide, a modulus operation is done to determine the index of the window that covers the neutron's energy. The fitting parameters from the window are applied to the various microscopic cross sections. Finally, using the start

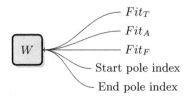

Fig. 5. Data structure representing a window.

Table 2. *RSBench* data structure summary

Nuclides tracked	355
Average resonances per nuclide	1,000
Average windows per nuclide	250
Total # of resonances	355,000
Cross section interaction types	4
Total size of cross section data structures	27 MB

and end pole indices of the window, the "pole" data structures are retrieved and used in several lengthy computations to determine their contributions to the various microscopic cross sections. Macroscopic cross sections are then accumulated. This process is summarized in Algorithm 2.

Algorithm 2. Multipole Macroscopic Cross Section Lookup

1: $R(m_p, E_p)$ ▷ randomly sample inputs
2: **for** $n \in m_p$ **do**   ▷ for each nuclide in input material
3:     Locate W Covering Energy E_p ▷ modulus operation
4:     Calculate Σ_l ▷ energy specific reaction channel values
5:     $\sigma_T \leftarrow W_T$ ▷ apply window's fitting function
6:     $\sigma_A \leftarrow W_A$
7:     $\sigma_F \leftarrow W_F$
8:     **for** $P \in W$ **do**   ▷ for each pole in window
9:        $\sigma_T \leftarrow P_{R_T}, \Sigma_l$ ▷ apply pole's residues
10:       $\sigma_A \leftarrow P_{R_A}$
11:       $\sigma_F \leftarrow P_{R_F}$
12:     **end for**
13:     $\sigma_E = \sigma_T - \sigma_A$
14:     $\Sigma \leftarrow \Sigma + \rho_n \cdot \sigma$ ▷ accumulate macro xs
15: **end for**

The equations used to assemble microscopic cross sections out of multipole resonance data are described in detail by Forget et al. [1]. Simplified forms of the 0 K multipole equations used by *RSBench*, are given in Eqs. 1, 2, and 3. Note that the effects of neutron spin are neglected under the assumption that all neutrons are spin zero, which in our experience does not impact performance. This simplification is made to reduce the programming complexity of the *RSBench* application, making it easier to instrument and port to new languages and systems, while still retaining a similar performance profile to the full multipole algorithm.

$$\sigma_x(E) = \frac{1}{E} \sum_{lj} \sum_{\lambda=1}^{N} \sum_{j=1}^{2(l+1)} \text{Re}\left[\frac{-ir_{x\lambda}^{(j)}}{p_\lambda^{(j)*} - \sqrt{E}}\right] \tag{1}$$

$$\sigma_t(E) = \sigma_p(E) + \frac{1}{E} \sum_{lj} \sum_{\lambda=1}^{N} \sum_{j=1}^{2(l+1)} \text{Re}\left[\exp(-i2\phi_l)\frac{-ir_{t\lambda}^{(j)}}{p_\lambda^{(j)*} - \sqrt{E}}\right] \tag{2}$$

where the potential cross section is given by

$$\sigma_p(E) = \sum_{lj} 4\pi\lambda^2 g_j \sin^2\phi_l \tag{3}$$

and where $r_{x\lambda}^{(j)}$ and $r_{t\lambda}^{(j)}$ are the residues for reaction x and total cross section around resonance λ, g_j is the spin statistical factor, $p_\lambda^{(j)*}$ is the complex conjugate of the pole, and ϕ_l is the phase shift. In this form, the cross sections can be computed by summations over angular momentum of the channel (l), channel spin (j), number of resonances (N) and number of poles associated to a given resonance type $2(l + 1)$.

3   Application

To investigate the performance profiles of our two MC transport cross section algorithms on existing systems, we carried out a series of tests using *RSBench* and *XSBench* on single node, multi-core, shared memory system. The system used was a single node consisting of two Intel Xeon E5-2650 octo-core CPUs for a total of 16 physical CPUs. All tests, unless otherwise noted, were run at 2.8 GHz using Intel Turbo Boost.

We performed a scaling study to determine performance improvements as additional cores were added. We ran both proxy applications with only a single thread to determine a baseline performance against which efficiency can be measured. Then, further runs were done to test each number of threads between 1 and 32. Efficiency is defined as

$$\text{Efficiency}_n = \frac{R_n}{R_1 \times n} \tag{4}$$

where n is the number of cores, R_n is the experimental calculation rate for n cores, and R_1 is the experimental calculation rate for one core.

The tests reveal that even for these proxy-applications of the MC transport algorithm, perfect scaling was not achievable. Figures 6 and 7 show that efficiency

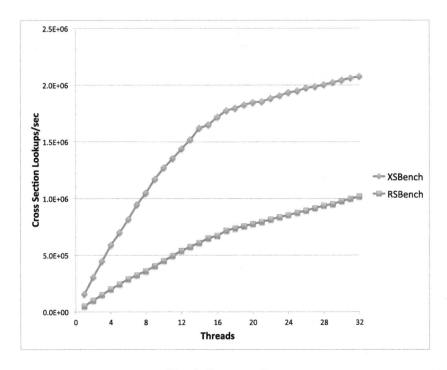

Fig. 6. Strong scaling

degraded gradually as more cores were used on the nodes. For the Xeon system, efficiency at 16 cores degraded to 69 % for *XSBench* and 83 % for *RSBench*.

One might reasonably conclude that 69 % or 83 % efficiency out to 16 cores is adequate speedup. However, next-generation node architectures are likely to require up to thousand-way on-node shared memory parallelism [7–10], and thus it is crucial to ascertain the cause of the observed degradation and the implications for greater levels of scalability. Considering nodes with 32, 64, 128, or 1024 shared memory cores and beyond, it cannot be taken for granted that performance will continue to improve. We thus seek to identify to the greatest extent possible which particular system resources are being exhausted, and how quickly, so that designers of future hardware systems as well as developers of future MC particle transport applications can avoid bottlenecks.

High performance computing (HPC) applications generally have several possible reasons for performance loss due to scaling:

1. FLOP bound – A CPU can only perform so many floating point operations per second.
2. Memory Bandwidth Bound – A finite amount of data can be sent between DRAM and the CPU.
3. Memory Latency Bound – An operation on the CPU that requires data be sent from the DRAM can take a long time to arrive.

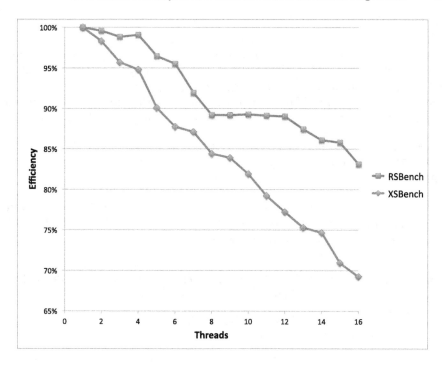

Fig. 7. Efficiency scaling

4. Inter-Node Communication Bound – Nodes working together on a problem may need to wait for data from other nodes, incurring large latency and bandwidth costs. This is not an issue for this application since we are focusing only on single node, shared-memory parallelism.

Given these potential candidates for bottlenecks, we aim to determine which exact subsystems are responsible for performance degradation by performing a series of studies to identify which specific resources our two kernels exhaust first.

4   Experiment and Results

To investigate the performance and resource utilization profiles of both proxy applications, and to determine the cause of multi-core scaling degradation, we performed a series of experiments. Each experiment involves varying a system parameter, monitoring hardware usage using performance counters, and/or altering a portion of the *XSBench* and *RSBench* codes. The following section presents descriptions, results, and preliminary conclusions for each experiment. For the purposes of simplicity, we concentrate our analysis on the Intel Xeon system described in Sect. 3. This allows us to get highly in-depth results as we are able to run experiments dealing with architecture-specific features and hardware counters.

4.1   Resource Usage

To better understand scaling degradation in our kernels, we implemented performance counting features into the source code of *XSBench* and *RSBench* using the Performance Application Programming Interface (PAPI) [17]. This allowed us to select from a large variety of performance counters (both preset and native to our particular Xeon chips). We collected data for many counters, including:

- `ix86arch::LLC_MISSES` - Last Level (L3) Cache Misses.
- `PAPI_TOT_CYC` - Total CPU Cycles.
- `PAPI_FP_INS` - Floating point instructions.

These raw performance counters allowed us to calculate a number of composite metrics, including bandwidth usage, FLOP utilization, and cache miss rate. Each of the metrics are discussed in the following subsections.

Bandwidth.   Consumption of available system bandwidth resources used by *XSBench* and *RSBench* is calculated using Eq. 5.

$$\text{Bandwidth} = \frac{\text{LLC\_MISSES} \times \text{Linesize}}{\text{PAPI\_TOT\_CYC}} \times \text{Clock (Hz)} \tag{5}$$

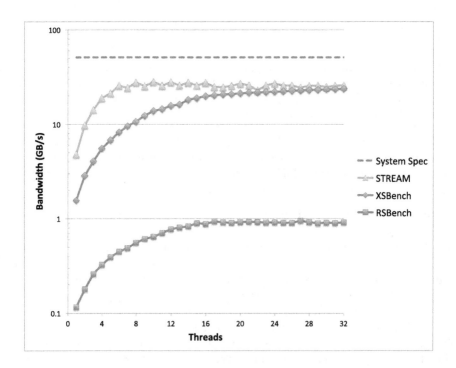

Fig. 8. Bandwidth usage scaling

Using Eq. 5, we collected the bandwidth usage for our proxy applications as run on varying numbers of cores, as shown in Fig. 8. Note that the maximum theoretically available bandwidth for the Xeon node is 51.2 GB/s [18]. Figure 8 shows that less than half the available bandwidth is ever used by either of our proxy applications, even when running at 32 threads per node[2].

There is, however, the question as to how much bandwidth is realistically usable on any given system. Even a perfectly constructed application that floods the memory system with easy, predictable loads is unlikely to be able to use the full system bandwidth. In order to determine what is actually usable on our Xeon system, we ran the *STREAM* benchmark, which measures "real world" bandwidth sustainable from ordinary user programs [19]. Results from this benchmark are shown in Fig. 8, and compared to *XSBench* and *RSBench*. As can be seen, *XSBench* converges with *STREAM*, leading us to believe that the classical cross section algorithm is bottlenecked by system bandwidth. In contrast, we find that the bandwidth usage of *RSBench* is much more conservative – using only 1 GB/s, a factor of over 20 less than what *XSBench* uses.

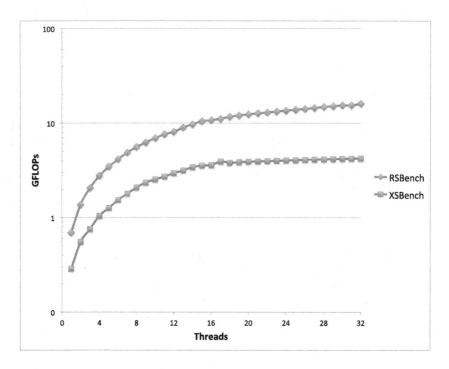

Fig. 9. FLOP usage

---

[2] The 16-core Xeon node used in our testing features hardware threading, supporting up to 32 threads per node.

Table 3. Performance Profile Comparison

Performance parameter	Classical (*XSBench*)	Multipole (*RSBench*)
Calculation rate (XS/s)	2,075,457	1,017,772
Bandwidth usage (GB/s)	23.7	0.91
Floating point usage (GFLOPs)	3.6	10.8
Cross section data structure size (MB)	5,734	27

FLOPs. Consumption of available system floating point resources used by *XSBench* and *RSBench* is calculated using Eq. 6.

$$\text{FLOPs} = \frac{\text{PAPI\_FP\_INS}}{\text{PAPI\_TOT\_CYC}} \times \text{Clock (Hz)} \qquad (6)$$

Using Eq. 6, we were able to determine the FLOP performance of our proxy applications, as shown in Fig. 9. We found that *XSBench* achieved at most 3.6 GFLOPs, while *RSBench* achieved three times the FLOP performance, at 10.8 GFLOPs.

5   Conclusions

We have performed an in-depth analysis of two different implementations of the MC neutron transport algorithm – the "classical" continuous energy cross section format (i.e., *XSBench*) and the multipole representation format (i.e., *RSBench*). We have also assessed the on-node scaling properties and memory contention issues of these algorithms in the context of a robust reactor physics calculation.

Through our investigations of the classical MC neutron cross section lookup algorithm, via *XSBench*, we found that it achieves bandwidth usage extremely close to the practical maximum of 25.8 GB/s when running 32 threads per node. At this point, the MC particle transport algorithm becomes limited by the available system bandwidth. Adding cores, hardware threads, or improving other latency masking techniques will not result in faster calculation rates; bandwidth must be increased for performance to increase for this algorithm.

We also found that the multipole algorithm (i.e., *RSBench*) uses over an order of magnitude less bandwidth (less than 1 GB/s) when compared to the classical approach while achieving over three times the FLOP performance. Scaling of multipole algorithm has been shown to be capable of better scaling (83 % efficiency at 16 cores per node vs. 69 % for the classical algorithm). On top of these impressive performance features, the multipole representation allows for a reduction in memory footprint of over two orders of magnitude.

Our performance analyses, summarized in Table 3, suggest that the multipole algorithm is purely FLOP bound and should scale well to hundreds or thousands of cores due to the algorithm's extremely low bandwidth requirements. Even though on today's systems the multipole algorithm only runs about half as fast, it has a significantly more desirable performance profile for scaling on next-generation systems, as processor cores per node and computational capacity are expected to greatly outpace increases in bandwidth to main memory. This is an important result, as the multipole method is not widely used in monte carlo transport codes yet exhibits an ideal performance profile for on-node scaling on many-core exascale architectures of the near future.

6   Future Work

There are additional capabilities that do not yet commonly exist in full-scale MC neutron transport algorithms, such as on-the-fly Doppler broadening to account for the material temperature dependence of cross sections, that we plan to implement in *XSBench* and *RSBench* for experimentation with various hardware architectures and features. This addition is predicted to enhance the advantages of the multipole algorithm as Doppler broadening is an inherently easier task when cross section data is already stored in the multipole format.

Acknowledgments. This work was supported by the Office of Advanced Scientific Computing Research, Office of Science, U.S. Department of Energy, under Contract DE-AC02-06CH11357. The submitted manuscript has been created by the University of Chicago as Operator of Argonne National Laboratory ("Argonne") under Contract DE-AC02-06CH11357 with the U.S. Department of Energy. The U.S. Government retains for itself, and others acting on its behalf, a paid-up, nonexclusive, irrevocable worldwide license in said article to reproduce, prepare derivative works, distribute copies to the public, and perform publicly and display publicly, by or on behalf of the Government.

References

1. Forget, B., Xu, S., Smith, K.: Direct Doppler broadening in Monte Carlo simulations using the multipole representation. Ann. Nucl. Energy **64**(C), 78–85 (2014)
2. Romano, P.K., Forget, B.: The OpenMC Monte Carlo particle transport code. Ann. Nucl. Energy **51**, 274–281 (2013)
3. Romano, P.K., Forget, B., Brown, F.B.: Towards scalable parallelism in Monte Carlo particle transport codes using remote memory access, pp. 17–21 (2010)
4. Siegel, A.R., Smith, K., Romano, P.K., Forget, B., Felker, K.G.: Multi-core performance studies of a Monte Carlo neutron transport code. Int. J. High Perform. Comput. Appl. **28**(1), 87–96 (2013)
5. Tramm, J., Siegel, A.R.: Memory bottlenecks and memory contention in multi-core Monte Carlo transport codes. In: Joint International Conference on Supercomputing in Nuclear Applications + Monte Carlo, Paris, October 2013. Argonne National Laboratory (2013)
6. Tramm, J.R., Siegel, A.R., Islam, T., Schulz, M.: XSBench - the development and verification of a performance abstraction for Monte Carlo reactor analysis. Presented at the PHYSOR 2014 - the role of reactor physics toward a sustainable future, Kyoto
7. Dosanjh, S., Barrett, R., Doerfler, D., Hammond, S., Hemmert, K., Heroux, M., Lin, P., Pedretti, K., Rodrigues, A., Trucano, T., Luitjens, J.: Exascale design space exploration and co-design. Future Gener. Comput. Syst. **30**, 46–58 (2013)

8. Attig, N., Gibbon, P., Lippert, T.: Trends in supercomputing: the European path to exascale. Comput. Phys. Commun. **182**(9), 2041–2046 (2011)

9. Rajovic, N., Vilanova, L., Villavieja, C., Puzovic, N., Ramirez, A.: The low power architecture approach towards exascale computing. J. Comput. Sci. **4**, 439–443 (2013)

10. Engelmann, C.: Scaling to a million cores and beyond: using light-weight simulation to understand the challenges ahead on the road to exascale. Future Gener. Comput. Syst. **30**, 59–65 (2013)

11. Romano, P.: OpenMC Monte Carlo code, January 2014. https://github.com/mit-crpg/openmc

12. Tramm, J.: XSBench: the Monte Carlo macroscopic cross section lookup benchmark, January 2014. https://github.com/jtramm/XSBench

13. Tramm, J.: RSBench: a mini-app to represent the multipole resonance representation lookup cross section algorithm, January 2014. https://github.com/jtramm/RSBench

14. Hoogenboom, J.E., Martin, W.R., Petrovic, B.: Monte Carlo performance benchmark for detailed power density calculation in a full size reactor core benchmark specifications. Ann. Arbor. **1001**, 42104–48109 (2010)

15. Romano, P.K., Siegel, A.R., Forget, B., Smith, K.: Data decomposition of Monte Carlo particle transport simulations via tally servers. J. Comput. Phys. **252**(C), 20–36 (2013)

16. Leppänen, J.: Two practical methods for unionized energy grid construction in continuous-energy Monte Carlo neutron transport calculation. Ann. Nucl. Energy **36**(7), 878–885 (2009)

17. ICL: PAPI - performance application programming interface, September 2013. http://icl.cs.utk.edu/papi/index.html

18. Intel: Xeon processor e5–2650 cpu specifications, September 2013. http://ark.intel.com/products/64590/

19. McCalpin, J.D.: Memory bandwidth and machine balance in current high performance computers. In: IEEE Computer Society Technical Committee on Computer Architecture (TCCA) Newsletter, December 1995, pp. 19–25 (1995)

Nek5000 with OpenACC

Jing Gong[1,3]([✉]), Stefano Markidis[1,3], Michael Schliephake[1,3], Erwin Laure[1,3],
Dan Henningson[2,3], Philipp Schlatter[2,3], Adam Peplinski[2,3], Alistair Hart[4],
Jens Doleschal[5], David Henty[6], and Paul Fischer[7]

[1] PDC Center for High Performance Computing, KTH Royal Institute
of Technology, Stockholm, Sweden
{gongjing,markidis,michs,erwinl}@pdc.kth.se
[2] Department of Mechanics, KTH Royal Institute of Technology, Stockholm, Sweden
{henningson,pschlatt,adam}@mech.kth.se
[3] The Swedish E-Science Center (SeRC), 100 44 Stockholm, Sweden
[4] Cray Exascale Research Initiative Europe, Edinburgh, UK
[5] ZIH, Technische Universität Dresden, Dresden, Germany
[6] Edinburgh Parallel Computing Centre, Edinburgh University, Edinburgh, UK
[7] Argonne National Laboratory, Lemont, IL, USA

Abstract. Nek5000 is a computational fluid dynamics code based on
the spectral element method used for the simulation of incompressible
flows. We follow up on an earlier study which ported the simplified version of Nek5000 to a GPU-accelerated system by presenting the hybrid
CPU/GPU implementation of the full Nek5000 code using OpenACC.
The matrix-matrix multiplication, the Nek5000 gather-scatter operator
and a preconditioned Conjugate Gradient solver have implemented using
OpenACC for multi-GPU systems. We report an speed-up of 1.3 on single
node of a Cray XK6 when using OpenACC directives in Nek5000. On 512
nodes of the Titan supercomputer, the speed-up can be approached to
1.4. A performance analysis of the Nek5000 code using Score-P and Vampir performance monitoring tools shows that overlapping of GPU kernels
with host-accelerator memory transfers would considerably increase the
performance of the OpenACC version of Nek5000 code.

Keywords: Nek5000 · OpenACC · GPU programming · Spectral element method

1 Introduction

Nek5000 is an open-source code for simulating incompressible flows [1]. The code
is widely used in a broad range of applications. The various research projects
at KTH Royal Institute of Technology Mechanics Department using Nek5000
include the study of turbulent pipe flow, the flow along airplane wings, a jet in
cross-flow and Lagrangian particle motion in complex geometries [2].

The Nek5000 discretization scheme is based on the spectral-element method [3].
In this approach, the incompressible Navier-Stokes equations are discretized in

S. Markidis and E. Laure (Eds.): EASC 2014, LNCS 8759, pp. 57–68, 2015.
DOI: 10.1007/978-3-319-15976-8_4

space by using high-order weighted residual techniques employing tensor-product polynomial bases. The tensor-product-based operator evaluation can be implemented as matrix-matrix products. This implementation makes it is possible to port the most time-consuming parts of the code into a GPU-accelerated system.

OpenACC [4,5] enables existing HPC application codes to run on accelerators with minimal source-code changes. This is done using compiler directives and API calls, with the compiler being responsible for generating optimized code and the user guiding performance only where necessary.

In [6] we presented a case study of porting NekBone, the simplified version of Nek5000, to a parallel GPU-accelerated system. In this paper, we follow on from the work developed in [6] and take advantage of the optimized results to port the full version of Nek5000 to a GPU-accelerated system.

The paper is organized as follows. We introduce the theoretical background in Sect. 2. In Sect. 3, the technique used to port the Nek5000 application onto a multi-GPU system is described in detail. In Sect. 4 we present the profiling and performance results from pipe simulations using the ported code. Finally, Sect. 5 summarizes the results and draws relevant conclusions.

2 Theoretical Background

In Nek5000 the incompressible Navier-Stokes equations in 3-D are written

$$\frac{\partial \mathbf{u}}{\partial t} + Re(\mathbf{u} \cdot \nabla \mathbf{u}) = -\nabla p + \nabla^2 \mathbf{u} + \mathbf{f}, \quad \text{in} \quad \Omega \in R^3$$
$$\nabla \cdot \mathbf{u} = 0 \quad \text{in} \quad \Omega \in R^3$$
(1)

where $\mathbf{u} = (u, v, w)$ is the velocity, p is the pressure and $\mathbf{f} = (f_x, f_y, f_z)$ is the forcing function.

The weak form of Eq. (1) is to find $\mathbf{v} = (u', v', w')$ and q such that

$$\int_\Omega \mathbf{v} \cdot \frac{\partial \mathbf{u}}{\partial t} d\Omega + Re \int_\Omega \mathbf{v} \cdot (\mathbf{u} \cdot \nabla \mathbf{u}) d\Omega = -\int_\Omega \mathbf{v} \cdot \nabla p d\Omega + \int_\Omega \mathbf{v} \cdot \nabla^2 \mathbf{u} d\Omega + \int_\Omega \mathbf{v} \cdot \mathbf{f} d\Omega$$
$$\int_\Omega q(\nabla \cdot \mathbf{u}) d\Omega = 0$$
(2)

When the spectral element method (SEM) [7] is employed in spatial discretization, the variable u (and v, w, p) and its first derivatives can be continuously represented as

$$u(x, y, z) = \sum_{i=0}^{N} \sum_{j=0}^{N} \sum_{k=0}^{N} u_{ijk} \psi_i(x) \psi_j(y) \psi_k(z)$$
$$\frac{\partial u(x, y, z)}{\partial x} = \sum_{i=0}^{N} \sum_{j=0}^{N} \sum_{k=0}^{N} u_{ijk} \frac{2}{|J|} \psi_i'(x) \psi_j(y) \psi_k(z)$$
(3)

for all elements $e = 1, 2, \cdots$. where ψ_{ijk} is the SEM function representation on the Gauss-Lobatto-Legendre points. The local tensor product form in Eq. (3) allows derivatives to be evaluated as matrix-matrix products or using matrix-matrix-based derivative evaluation (for more detail see [7]).

Nek5000 supports two distinct algorithms P_N-P_N and P_N-P_{N-2} for solving Eq. (4). In this paper, we focus on the P_N-P_N algorithm: we first discretize in time and then take the continuous divergence of momentum equation to obtain a Poisson equation for pressure. When high-order backward-difference schemes (BDFk) in time are used, the discretized matrix form of the Navier-Stokes equation can be written

$$
\begin{bmatrix} H & 0 & 0 & 0 \\ 0 & H & 0 & 0 \\ 0 & 0 & H & 0 \\ 0 & 0 & 0 & A \end{bmatrix} \begin{bmatrix} u_1^n \\ u_2^n \\ u_3^n \\ p^n \end{bmatrix} = \begin{bmatrix} f_1^n \\ f_2^n \\ f_3^n \\ g^n \end{bmatrix} \tag{4}
$$

where $H = \frac{1}{Re}A + \frac{\beta_0}{\Delta t}B$ is the discrete Helmholtz operator and A is the symmetric positive-definite Laplace operator. Note that f^n accounts for all the terms known prior to time t^n. The resultant linear system is computed with Conjugate Gradient (CG) linear solver accelerated with convenient preconditioners.

3 Accelerating and Optimizing Nek5000 on Multi-GPU

3.1 Profiling Analysis

An initial performance profiling of the Nek5000 application on a single CPU was carried out using the Cray Performance Analysis Tool (CrayPAT) profiler. The goal of this profiling work was to identify which subroutines are the most time consuming and can provide enough workload to exploit GPU computational power. The profiling table below shows the profiling results.

Time%		Time	Imb. Time	Imb. Time%	Calls	Group Function
100.0%		191.107502	--	--	44148206.0	Total
99.3%		189.766300	--	--	42866946.0	USER
33.5%		63.981577	--	--	30584418.0	mxf10_
19.6%		37.490228	--	--	2450.0	axhelm_
9.7%		18.620119	--	--	40.0	cggo_
8.8%		16.788978	--	--	5118400.0	mxf12_
8.3%		15.881574	--	--	10.0	hmh_gmres_
4.4%		8.406132	--	--	914.0	h1mg_schwarz
2.4%		4.595712	--	--	914.0	hsmg_do_fast_
2.4%		4.544659	--	--	457.0	h1mg_solve_
1.4%		2.630254	--	--	2924800.0	mxf6_

Profiling results of Nek5000 on single node with the CrayPAT profile

It is clear from the profiling results that the subroutines `mxf6`, `mxf10` and `mxf12` for calculating the matrix-matrix product required approximately 43.7 % of the time. Other subroutines (`axhelm`, `cggo`, `hmh_gmres`, `h1mg_schwarz`, `hsmg_do_fast` and `h1mg_solve`) for solving a preconditioned CG solver required approximately 46.8 % of the total time. The matrix-matrix multiplication and the linear algebra solvers dominate the execution time of Nek5000.

3.2 Matrix-Matrix Production

The implementation of matrix-matrix multiplication presented in Ref. [6] was followed. The subroutine axhelm was implemented with OpenACC directives as shown in the code below. The code on the left side of the table is the original Nek5000 code, while the code in the right part of the table is the new implementation using OpenACC.

```
                      !$ACC  DATA PRESENT(u,w)
                      !$ACC& PRESENT(D,g)
                      !$ACC  PARALLEL LOOP COLLAPSE(4)
                      !$ACC& GANG WORKER VECTOR
                      !$ACC& VECTOR_LENGTH(128)
do e=1,nel            do e=1,nel
   call mxm(...)         do k=1,n
   do j=1,n             do j=1,n
      call mxm(...) =>     do i=1,n
   enddo                     temp = 0
   call mxm(...)      !$ACC SEQ
enddo                      do l=1,n
                             temp = temp + D(i,l)*u(l,j,k,e)
                           enddo
                           w(i,j,k,e) = g(i,j,k,e)*temp
                         enddo
                       enddo
                     enddo
                   enddo
```

Optimized OpenACC derivatives for the matrix matrix production.

3.3 Gather-Scatter Operator

In the traditional finite element methods, the global matrix is typically assembled by the distinct nodes associated with the global indices. However, in Nek5000, the linear system is written as $A_L u_L = b$, where u_L is the vector of values for each node associated with local indices based on elements.

As an example, a mesh of 4 elements in 2-D is shown in Fig. 1. In this mesh there are 9 global nodes $(0, \ldots, 8)$ and 16 local nodes $(0, \ldots, 15)$. One global node may correspond to several local nodes. The solution of the linear system

$A_L u_L = b$ is neither reasonable nor converged, because the values of u_L on a particular global node that is shared with different local nodes are usually inconsistent, e.g.

$$u_L^4 \neq u_L^7 \neq u_L^{11} \neq u_L^{13}$$

on the shared global node 4. The *gather-scatter* method is employed to remove the effect of such inconsistencies in every time-step. The method firstly summarizes all values on the same global node and calculates the average, and then redistributes the value to the original local node. The gather-scatter method can be denoted in matrix form as

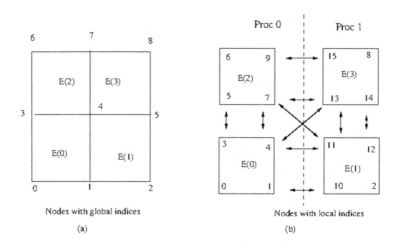

Fig. 1. A mesh of four elements in 2-D

$$\tilde{u}_L = Q^T u_G = Q^T Q u_L \tag{5}$$

where the Boolean matrix Q is the gather operator and its transform Q^T is the scatter operator. Notice that matrix Q is not explicitly implemented in Nek5000, instead a local-global map `lgl(local_index, global_index)` is used. The local-global map for the mesh in Fig. 2 is

```
          procs: 0  0  0  0  0  0 || 1  1  1  1  1  1
 local_indices: 1  3  5  4  7  9 || 10 11 13 12 14 15
global_indices: 1  3  3  4  4  7 || 1  4  4  5  5  7
```

To reduce MPI global communication, those nodes that share a global index in the same processes are summed locally and then exchanged with other processors. For example, the parallel version of the gather-scatter operator (**gs_op**) for the value on global node 4 shared with local nodes 4, 7, 11, and 13 is

$$u_G^4 = \frac{u_L^4 + u_L^7}{2} \quad \text{(Proc 0)}, \qquad u_G^4 = \frac{u_L^{11} + u_L^{13}}{2} \quad \text{(Proc 1)}$$

$$u_G^4 = \frac{u_G^4 \text{ (on Proc 0)} + u_G^4 \text{ (on Proc 1)}}{2}, \quad \text{(MPI gs\_op)}$$

$$\tilde{u}_L^4 = \tilde{u}_L^7 = u_G^4 \quad \text{(Proc 0)}, \qquad \tilde{u}_L^{11} = \tilde{u}_L^{13} = u_G^4 \quad \text{(Proc 1)}$$

This allows us to adapt the modified gather-scatter method for OpenACC as shown below.

```
unew_l = u_l
! u_g = Q u_l Local Gather
!$ACC PARALLEL LOOP
 u_g = 0
 do i = 1, nl
    li = lgl(1,i)
    gi = lgl(2,i)
    u_g(gi) = u_g(gi)+u_l(li)
 enddo

gs_op(u_g,1,1,0) ! MPI

! u_l = Q^T u_g Local Scatter
!$ACC PARALLEL LOOP
do i = 1, nl
    li = lgl(1,i)
    gi = lgl(2,i)
    unew_l(li) = u_g(gi)
enddo
```

*The modified **gs_op** operator with local gather and scatter*

3.4 Preconditioned Conjugate Gradient Solver

The OpenACC code of the preconditioned conjugate gradient solver CG for calculating the pressure field is shown below.

```
!$ACC  DATA PRESENT(r,w,z,d,p,h1,h2)
!$ACC& PRESENT(mask,mult,nel,ktype)
  do iter=1,niter
     call fdm_h1_acc(z,r,d,mask,mult,nel,ktype,w)
     call crs_solve_h1_acc (w,r)
     call add2_acc    (z,w,n)
     call add2s1_acc  (p,z,beta,n)
     call axhelm_acc  (w,p,h1,h2,imsh,isd)
     call gs_op       (w,nx1,ny1,nz1)
     call col2_acc    (w,mask,n)
```

```
      rho  = glsc3_acc(w,p,mult,n)
      alpha=rtz1/rho; alphm=-alpha
      call add2s2_acc (x,p,alpha,n)
      call add2s2_acc (r,w,alphm,n)
   enddo
```

The OpenACC version of the preconditioned Conjugate Gradients solver. In the OpenACC implementation, the subroutine `gs_op` needs to be called once to exchange the interface data between GPUs.

4   Performance Results

A Nek5000 simulation of the flow in a straight pipe with 400 elements and polynomials of order 10 was used to test the performance of the Nek5000 with OpenACC simulation. These tests were carried out on a Cray XK6 consisting of four compute nodes with a 2.1 GHz AMD Interlagos 16-core processor, 16 GB memory and one Kepler K20 GPU. The version 8.1 of the Cray Compilation Environment (CCE) supporting OpenACC was used. The execution times per iteration with different orders of polynomial using the CG linear solver and Schwarz preconditioner are compared in Table 1. The speed-up achieved using OpenACC directives is 1.3 with 15th order polynomial on a single GPU compared to single nodes with 16 CPU cores. In addition, the Nek5000 code with OpenACC directives have been profiled with CrayPAT. The profiling results are shown below. The execution time of the subroutine axhelm reduces to 2.1 s (37.5 s in the original Nek5000) when using OpenACC. The subroutine mxf10 reduces to 10.7 s (63.9 s in the original Nek5000).

Table 1. Execution time in seconds with different orders of polynomial using the CG linear solver and Schwarz preconditioner. 400 elements and the CG solver with Schwarz preconditiones were used.

Order	1 node (s)	1 GPU (s)	Speed-up
12th	5.6	6.3	0.89
13th	8.7	8.7	1.0
14th	11.9	11.2	1.1
15th	15.5	11.8	1.3

```
Time%     |      Time  | Imb.  | Imb.   |     Calls  |Group
          |           | Time  | Time%  |            |Function
 100.0%   | 30.070742 |   --  |    --  | 6545592.0  |Total
|-----------------------------------------------------------
|  96.0%  | 28.866030 |   --  |    --  | 5342163.0  |USER
```

```
||---------------------------------------------------------------
|| 35.7% | 10.748494 |    -- |     -- | 4998018.0 |mxf10_
||  8.3% |  2.495744 |    -- |     -- |      30.0 |char_conv1_
||  7.0% |  2.103028 |    -- |     -- |     142.0 |axhelm_
||  6.9% |  2.070768 |    -- |     -- |     228.0 |convop_fst_3d_
||  3.6% |  1.093646 |    -- |     -- |    1028.0 |glsc3
||  3.5% |  1.047823 |    -- |     -- |     390.0 |hsmg_do_fast_
||  1.9% |  0.571661 |    -- |     -- |      10.0 |makeuf_
||  1.4% |  0.429575 |    -- |     -- |    3079.0 |vlsc3_acc_
||  1.3% |  0.392988 |    -- |     -- |      50.0 |chktcg1_
||  1.3% |  0.380326 |    -- |     -- |       1.0 |eigenv_
||  1.3% |  0.378630 |    -- |     -- |     390.0 |hsmg_tnsr1_3d_
||=============================================================
|   2.3% |  0.701164 |    -- |     -- |    3609.0 |LAPACK
||---------------------------------------------------------------
|   2.3% |  0.701164 |    -- |     -- |    3609.0 | dsygv_
||=============================================================
|   1.6% |  0.475458 |    -- |     -- | 1181795.0 |BLAS
|=============================================================
```

Profiling results of Nek5000 with OpenACC on a single node

In addition, we report the initial results for the multi-GPU OpenACC version of Nek5000 on the Titan supercomputer. This is a Cray XK7 supercomputer, consisting of 18, 688 AMD Opteron 6274 16-core CPUs and 18, 688 Nvidia Tesla K20X GPUs. For the tests on Titan, a case with a total of 36, 400 elements and 16th-order polynomials (for a total of approximately 149 M points) was used [10]. Table 2 shows the execution times per iteration with 512 CPU nodes and 512 GPUs. When using 512 nodes with 512 GPUs on Titan supercomputer, the speed-up reduces to 1.39.

Table 2. Execution time per iteration in seconds on 512 Titan supercomputer nodes using only CPU and on 512 GPUs. 36400 elements and 16th order polynomial were used.

512 nodes (s)	512 GPU (s)	Speed-up
7.02	5.07	1.39

4.1 Performance Analysis with Score-P and Vampir

A more detailed application performance analysis of Nek5000 with OpenACC was completed by tracing Nek5000 with the Score-P [8] performance monitoring tool. The tracing of the GPU kernels was carried out by intercepting the underlying CUDA calls via the CUDA profiling interface CUPTI. The monitoring was completed on one node of Titan at Oak Ridge National Laboratory. The visualization of the resulting monitoring information was done with the performance visualizer Vampir [9].

Figure 2 shows the color-coded application run-time behavior over the whole run-time of 151.93 s for the CPU process (Master thread) and the GPU stream (CUDA[0:2]). The figure shows the three main phases of the Nek5000 code nek_init (initialization), nek_solve (main calculation), and nek_post (post-processing). These three phases can be easily distinguished by comparing the different color-coded patterns in the timeline of the CPU process. All compiler generated OpenACC kernels are grouped in CUDA Kernel. The overall run-time of these kernels was 102.416 s (67.41 % of the application run-time) while the GPU was idle for the rest of the time (32.59 % of the application run-time).

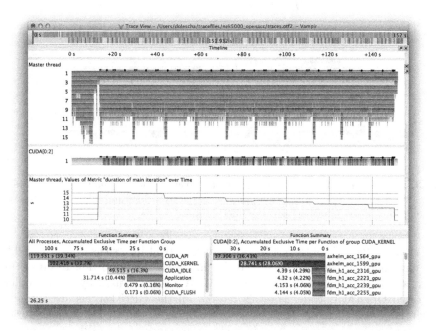

Fig. 2. Function-based, color-coded visualization of the CPU process and GPU stream over the full application run-time and additional statistics of the groups of the functions and the GPU kernels. In the timeline of the metric duration of the main iteration the dynamic behavior of the duration of each iteration over is visualized.

Figure 3 shows the zoomed-in, color-coded run-time behavior of the application during the main calculation phase over ten Nek5000 computational iterations. It shows that the idle time of the GPU was reduced in comparison to the whole run-time to 25.35 %. The ten different iterations have different duration, varying from 15.16 s (first iteration) to 12.32 s (tenth iteration). This can be seen in the metric timeline of the metric duration over time.

The main GPU kernels are the matrix-matrix multiplication in the subroutine axhelm taking 36.43 % of the run-time and a kernel that consumes 28.06 % of

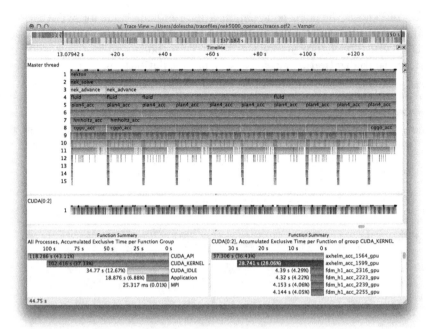

Fig. 3. Zoomed-in, function-based, color-coded visualization of the CPU process and GPU stream of the main calculation phase with ten iterations and additional statistics of the groups of the functions and the GPU kernels.

the run-time. 24.68 % of the GPU run-time was spent in kernels that are used to do a mapping between the coarse and the fine mesh. An important result of this analysis is that it shows that only one CUDA stream is used by the compiler-generated OpenACC code. For this reason, all the GPU kernels are executed sequentially and therefore there is no overlapping of the CUDA kernels during the execution. As a result, the achieved performance of the GPU relies on the degree of vectorization of each OpenACC kernel, i.e. how many massively parallel threads can be created within each kernel. The main CPU process routine is a synchronization of CUDA called cuda_StreamSynchronize and uses in fact 90 % of the CPUs application run-time. This function is part of the group CUDA_API, which includes all CUDA API calls monitored on the CPU process and was introduced by the compiler and used in the OpenACC regions.

Figure 4 presents the color-coded visualization of the first iteration on the Nek5000 simulation. This iteration has a duration of 15.154 s and the idle time of the GPU for this phase is 3.441 s (22.7 %). The CPU process spent most of its time in the CUDA synchronization routine (light blue color in Fig. 4). The most time consuming kernels of the GPU are again the matrix-matrix computation with 4.631 s and respectively 3.363 s. In future work, to improve the performance of Nek5000 with OpenACC by decreasing the GPU idle time, it will be important to use overlapping of kernels and/or host-device memory transfers.

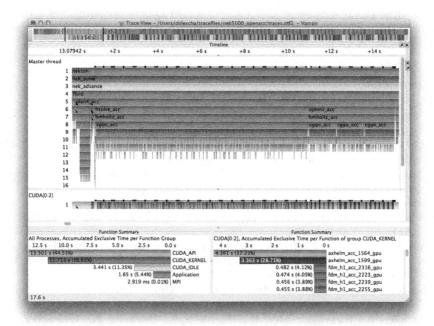

Fig. 4. Zoomed-in, function-based, color-coded visualization of the CPU process and GPU stream of the first iteration and additional statistics of the groups of the functions and the GPU kernels.

5   Conclusions

The full Nek5000 code has been ported to multi-GPU systems using OpenACC compiler directives. The work focused on porting the most time-consuming parts of Nek5000 to the GPU systems, namely the matrix-matrix multiplication and the preconditioned CG linear solver. The gather-scatter method with MPI operations has been redesigned in order to decrease the amount of data to transfer between host and accelerator. A speed-up of 1.3 times was found on a single node of a Cray XK6 when using OpenACC. On 512 nodes of the Titan supercomputer, the speed-up can be approached to 1.6 times. A performance analysis of the Nek5000 code using Score-P and Vampir performance monitoring tools was carried out. This study showed that overlapping of GPU kernels with host-accelerator memory transfers would largely increase the performance of the OpenACC version of Nek5000 code. This will be part of future research.

Acknowledgment. This research has received funding from the Swedish e-Science Research Centre (SeRC) and the European Community's Seventh Framework Programme (ICT-2011.9.13) under Grant Agreement no. 287703, cresta.eu. We are grateful for the computing time that was made available to us on the Raven system at Cray and on the Titan supercomputer at Oak Ridge National Laboratory within the INCITE program. We would also like to thank Dr. George K. El Khoury for the benchmark used in the paper.

References

1. Fischer, P.F., Lottes J.W., Kerkemeier S.G.: Nek5000 web page. http://nek5000.mcs.anl.gov
2. The second nek5000 Users and Development Meeting, Zurich, Switzerland. http://nek5000.mcs.anl.gov/index.php/Usermeeting2012
3. Patera, A.T.: A spectral element method for fluid dynamics: laminar flow in a channel expansion. J. Comput. Phys. **54**(3), 468–488 (1984)
4. OpenACC standard, June 2013. http://www.openacc-standard.org
5. Ansaloni R., Hart A.: Cray's approach to heterogeneous computing. In: PARCO (2011)
6. Markidis, S., Gong, J., Schliephake, M., Laure, E., Hart, A., Henty, D., Heisey, K., Fischer, P.F.: OpenACC acceleration of Nek5000, spectral element code. Int. J. High Perform. Comput. Appl. (IJHPCA)
7. Deville, M.O., Fischer, P.F., Mund, E.H.: High-Order Method for Incompressible Fluid Flow. Cambridge University Press, Cambridge (2002)
8. Knüpfer, A., Rössel, C., Mey, D., Biersdorff, S., Diethelm, K., Eschweiler, D., Geimer, M., Gerndt, M., Lorenz, D., Malony, A., Nagel, W.E., Oleynik, Y., Philippen, P., Saviankou, P., Schmidl, D., Shende, S., Tschüter, R., Wagner, M., Wesarg, B., Wolf, F.: Tools for High Performance Computing 2011, pp. 79–91. Springer, Heidelberg (2012). doi:10.1007/978-3-642-31476-6_7
9. Knüpfer, A., Brunst, H., Doleschal, J., Jurenz, M., Lieber, M., Mickler, H., Müller, M.S., Nagel, W.E.: The vampir performance analysis tool set. In: Resch, M., Keller, R., Himmler, V., Krammer, B., Schulz, A. (eds.) Tools for High Performance Computing, pp. 139–155. Springer, Heidelberg (2008)
10. Schlatter, P., Khoury, G.K.E.: Turbulent flow in pipes. PDC Newsletter, no. 1 (2012)

Auto-tuning an OpenACC Accelerated Version of Nek5000

Luis Cebamanos[1]($\boxtimes$), David Henty[1], Harvey Richardson[2], and Alistair Hart[2]

[1] EPCC, The University of Edinburgh, Edinburgh, UK
{1.cebamanos,d.henty}@epcc.ed.ac.uk
[2] Cray Inc, Centre of Excellence, Edinburgh, UK
{harveyr,ahart}@cray.com

Abstract. Accelerators and, in particular, Graphics Processing Units (GPUs) have emerged as promising computing technologies which may be suitable for the future Exascale systems. However, the complexity of their architectures and the impenetrable structure of some large applications makes the hand-tuning algorithms process more challenging and unproductive. On the contrary, auto-tuning technology has appeared as a solution to this problems since it can address the inherent complexity of the latest and future computer architectures. By auto-tuning, an application may be optimised for a target platform by making automated optimal choices. To exploit this technology on modern GPUs, we have created an auto-tuned version of Nek5000 based on OpenACC directives which has demonstrated to obtained improved results over a hand-tune optimised version of the same computation kernels. This paper focuses on a particular role for auto-tuning Nek5000 to utilise a massively parallel GPU accelerated system based on OpenACC directive to adapt the Nek5000 code for the Exascale computation.

Keywords: Computational fluids · Nek5000 · OpenACC · GPU · Auto-tuning

1 Introduction

The use of Graphics Processing Units (GPUs) for general purpose in High Performance Computing (HPC) has been dramatically increased in recent years. GPUs are nowadays broadly used to solve computational problems in a wide range of areas such as engineering, computational chemistry or physics [1,2]. They have gained a vast popularity as a cost-effective platform in High Performance Computing and Scientific applications in the recent years due to their parallel computation capabilities and computational power. Modern GPUs are able to run thousands of hardware threads concurrently which allows applications to decompose their workloads into the threads without introducing a significant overhead [3]. The market leader of these devices at present is NVIDIA with their current generation Tesla [4] GPUs installed in a large number of petascale

© Springer International Publishing Switzerland 2015
S. Markidis and E. Laure (Eds.): EASC 2014, LNCS 8759, pp. 69–81, 2015.
DOI: 10.1007/978-3-319-15976-8_5

HPC systems. Motivated by this we choose to investigate the performance of our experiments on the Tesla architecture.

One of the major drawbacks of programming NVIDIA GPUs has been that the programming model, CUDA [5], is not a recognised standard and is completely proprietary to NVIDIA. CUDA (Compute Unified Device Architecture) is a parallel computing architecture developed by NVIDIA Corporation and is the computing engine in NVIDIA GPUs that is accessible to software developers [7]. Although there has been a large volume of research into porting HPC kernels to GPUs [6,7], the HPC community is nervous about investing substantial software development effort in converting applications to use a programming language that is not portable between different architectures. Although significant additions for accelerators have been included to the existing OpenMP standard [8] for shared-memory directives, this is likely to be a long process until the technology reaches maturity. To address this, a number of HPC hardware and software vendors got together to produce an interim standard for accelerator directives, OpenACC [9], based on their own experiences and guided by the direction of the OpenMP efforts. OpenACC allows the application developer to express the offloading of data and computations to GPUs, such that the porting process for legacy CPU based applications can be significantly simplified [10].

In the past, OpenACC has already demonstrated to work well with some computational codes which implement relatively simple operations [11,12]. Furthermore, OpenACC has already been successfully introduced in Nek5000 [13], a more computationally-demanding code that implements a Computational Fluid Dynamics (CFD) solver based on the spectral element method. In this paper we report an extensive auto-tuning study of a skeleton application of Nek5000, Nekbone [14]. The previous OpenACC accelerated code by Markidis, S. et al. [15] is used as the base to compare our results. The performance results of auto-tuning Nekbone using OpenACC for a single GPU are presented.

In Sect. 2, we present the necessary background information where Nekbone, Nek5000 are briefly described. Furthermore, a stand-alone kernel benchmark based on the computation of Nekbone is presented in Sects. 2.2. In Sect. 3, we briefly describe the structure of the implemented OpenACC kernels. Section 4 shows the performance the results of different implementations. Finally, Sect. 5 summarizes the results and draws relevant conclusions.

2 Background

2.1 Nek5000

Nek5000 is a scalable open-source code which simulates incompressible flow with thermal and passive scalar transport. Its discretization scheme is based on spectral element methods [17] and covers a wide range of application areas, such as nuclear reactor modeling, astrophysics, climate modeling, combustion and biofluids [16]. The code is written in Fortran, C and uses Message Passing Interface (MPI) for message passing and some LAPACK routines for eigenvalue computation.

The core computational kernel of Nek5000 is dominated by a large number of matrix-matrix operations that could be implemented by a call to the standard DGEMM function from level 3 of the BLAS library [18]. However, the particular calculation required in Nek5000 has a number of distinguishing features:

1. It requires multiplications between a large number of independent small matrices as opposed to a small number of multiplications of large matrices. This means that memory bandwidth is stressed as well as floating-point performance, which is not the case for a typical large DGEMM test case.
2. A wide range of matrix sizes are employed although all are small.
3. The matrices are not always square: for a given value of N the benchmark has three cases with matrices of size N x N, N^2 x N and N x N^2. The values of N range between 1 and 24.

2.2   Nekbone

Nekbone is a standard program provided with the Nek5000 application and it has been configured to capture the basic structure and user interface of the extensive Nek5000 software. It requires F77 and C compilers and it has been tested and supported by IBM, Intel, PGI Portland and GNU compilers although other compilers may be used. Nek5000 is a complex Navier-Stokes solver based on the spectral element method, whereas Nekbone solves a Helmholtz equation in a box using the same method. Nekbone exposes the main computational kernel to reveal the essential elements of the algorithm-architectural coupling that is relevant to Nek5000 [14], therefore our work here focuses only on the optimization and auto-tuning process of Nekbone since it is understood that any improvement achieved on the computational structure of Nekbone could also be applied to Nek5000.

2.3   Stand-Alone Kernel Benchmark

A standard program that executes some low level benchmarks without requiring any input files is supplied with the Nek5000 distribution. It runs both computation and (matrix-matrix operations) and communication (ping-pong, reduction, etc.) kernels. Although it would have been possible to comment out the communication operations of the benchmark, it was finally decided to extract the minimal amount of code needed to run the calculation benchmark. For the purpose of this investigation, new kernels were to be added therefore a verification routine was introduced to ensure correctness. A reference solution is computed using the simplest version of the kernels. All subsequent results are compared to this reference by computing the RMS difference, and if this exceeds a certain tolerance (set to 1.0^{-12}), then an error is reported. All calculations are done in double precision, although this is actually achieved by promoting reals to doubles using compiler flags.

The existing DGEMM benchmark originally had the following structure:

1. Declare three arrays A, B and C, each containing M matrices
2. Loop over a high number of repetitions for timing purposes

- Loop over $i = 1, 2, ..., M$
  - Compute matrix-matrix multiplication $C(i) = A(i) * B(i)$
3. End repetitions

The sizes of the individual matrices are determined by the value of N, which corresponds to the order of the spectral elements in Nek5000. The benchmark considers three cases for a given value of N each of which uses matrices of different dimension. The three test cases of $C = A * B$ are:

1. N^2 x N matrix times N x N matrix equals N^2 x N matrix
2. N x N matrix times N x N matrix equals N x N matrix
3. N x N matrix times N x N^2 matrix equals N x N^2 matrix

The value of M is related to the size of the problem that is being solved in Nek5000. In the kernel benchmark, a fixed amount of memory comprising $NFLOAT$ floating-point numbers is declared. The value of M is then set to fill this array with as many matrices as possible, i.e. for each case:

- Case 1 $\rightarrow M = NFLOAT/(N^3)$
- Case 2 $\rightarrow M = NFLOAT/(N^2)$
- Case 3 $\rightarrow M = NFLOAT/(N^3)$

This means that the inner loop always has roughly the same number of floating-point operations of order M x N^3. Although there is a factor of N more matrices for case 2, the matrices themselves are smaller so each matrix multiplication has corresponding a factor of N fewer floating-point operations.

The kernels included in the benchmark implement a simple computation as it is shown in Algorithm 1.

Algorithm 1. Naïve matrix-matrix computation

```
do j = 1, n3
   do i = 1, n1

     c( i, j ) = 0.0

     do k = 1, n2
        c ( i, j ) = c ( i, j ) + a ( i, k ) * b ( k, j )
     end do

   end do
end do
```

In order to investigate the performance of Nekbone through the use of the mentioned extracted stand-alone benchmark it is important to highlight the how the kernel benchmarks relate to the Nekbone computational kernels. The number of elements, nel, corresponds to setting a particular value of floating-point value, $NFLOAT$, in the kernel benchmarks. As each element requires N^3 storage, $nel = NLFOAT/N^3$. In Nekbone, updating a single element requires six kernel calls: two separate calls for each of the three cases. These cases actually correspond to operations across different spatial dimensions of the 3D elements. In the Nekbone kernel, the computational load is equally distributed between the three kernel cases. In terms of the number of elements nel, the value of M in the benchmark is set as $M = nel$ for cases 1 and 3, and $M = nel * N$ for case 2. The core operation in Nekbone is implemented by a routine called ax_e and considering that the repetition of its inner operations are not relevant in terms of performance and neither the order of the calls to the three different cases, we could re-write it in the following form:

> **loop** $e = 1$ **to** nel
>> *Update* **e** *using kernel case 1*
>> **loop** $k = 1$ **to** N
>>> *Update* **e** *using kernel case 2*
>> **end loop**
>> *Update* **e** *using kernel case 3*
> **end loop**

Given that nel and N are likely to be fixed for many runs of Nek5000 (as they correspond to the basic discretization parameters of the simulation) the way for a user to optimize Nekbone performance using the benchmark is as follows:

1. Set $NFLOAT$ based on nel; the precise choice is not important with respect to performance, e.g. assuming that nel is large then it only has to be large enough to ensure that data is read from memory and is not cache resident.
2. Run the benchmark and find the routine with the best harmonic mean performance across all three cases.
3. Compile that single version and use in all calls.

3   OpenACC Kernels

Since GPUs require many independent floating-point operations in order to exploit massive parallelism, and a single kernel do not provide sufficient parallelism it was decided that the accelerated kernels would have to operate on a whole array of elements at once. Furthermore, the kernel benchmarks were updated to perform as in Nekbone. In Nekbone one of the matrices (either A or B) was actually fixed throughout the loop. The new accelerated Nekbone kernel has the following form:

- Call accelerated kernel case 1 for $C(i) = A(i) * B$ (vector length = nel)
- Call accelerated kernel case 2 for $C(i) = A(i) * B$ (vector length = nel * N)
- Call accelerated kernel case 3 for $C(i) = A * B(i)$ (vector length = nel)

Over 10 different implementations of each kernel have been included in the benchmark providing many different computation paths for the Nekbone kernel and exploring the following types of optimizations:

- specific hard-coded versions for different values of n1, n2 and n3 so that these are constant at compile time;

- different loop orderings;
- loop unrolling;
- hand tiling into blocks for better cache reuse;
- calls to DGEMM routines;
- matrix values stored explicitly in temporary scalars;
- loop collapsing.

Therefore, our new kernel routines using OpenACC accelerated code could be re-written in the following form:

Call *OpenACC kernel case 1*
Call *OpenACC kernel case 2*
Call *OpenACC kernel case 3*
Update values
Call *OpenACC update kernel case 1*
Call *OpenACC update kernel case 2*
Call *OpenACC update kernel case 3*

and the new OpenACC kernels included now implement variations of OpenACC optimized code

---

Algorithm 2. Simple OpenACC matrix-matrix computation

```
!$acc parallel loop present(a,b,c) private(i,j,k)
do j = 1, n3
    do i = 1, n1
#ifdef SCALAR
    tmp  = 0.0
#else
    c( i, j ) = 0.0
#ifdef SCALAR
    tmp  = tmp  + a( i, k ) * b ( k, j )
#else
    do k = 1, n2
        c ( i, j ) = c ( i, j ) + a ( i, k ) * b ( k, j )
    end do
#ifdef SCALAR
    c( i, j ) = tmp
#endif
    end do
end do
```

3.1   Auto-tuning Technology

In the interest of obtaining the best performance results of Nekbone here we employed auto-tuning technology developed under the EU CRESTA research project [25]. As part of a wider study to define a domain-specific language (DSL) appropriate for auto-tuning aspects of parallel applications a mock-up implementation was developed within the project. This implementation can explore a tuning parameter space by repeatedly building and running an application. The best run is chosen using a metric obtained from the program execution and currently this is done by exhaustive search. To accomplish a tuning run the source is appropriately preprocessed or compiled and an optimization process organized. The tuning session is controlled by DSL either from a global configuration file or embedded in application source.

The DSL is a component of an auto-tuning framework and at the highest level it is assumed that this framework can optimize an application over a set of tuning parameters. Some parameters we term here *scenario characterization parameters* and these may for example, map to input parameters relating to problem size. This is illustrated in Fig. 1.

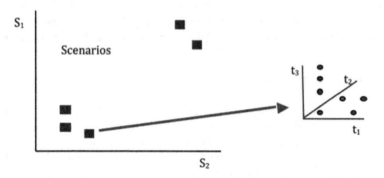

Fig. 1. Scenario and tuning spaces

For each scenario, we aim to pick the best values for a set of tuning parameters (see Fig. 1: t1, t2, and t3). The tuning parameters will relate to build and runtime optimization choices which we can choose to give for example the best runtime. At its simplest, the auto-tuner framework can optimize over the tuning parameters, at the most complex it can build routines and applications choosing the best tuning parameters for a set of scenario characterization parameters.

The structure for a DSL tuning parameters configuration file can be seen as follow:

```
begin parameters
  begin typing
    <type-entity>
  end typing

  begin constraints
    <constraint-entity>
  end constraints

  begin collections
    <collection-entity>
  end collections
```

```
begin dependencies
  depend: <depend-list>
end dependencies
end parameters
```

The *typing* section allows parameters to be typed as int, real or label. The set of allowed values of a parameter are defined in the *constraints* section. This supports specific sets of values, ranges, parameter relationships and legality constraints. Parameters may be grouped into *collections* and the *dependency* section allows us to say which parameters should be treated as dependent where depend-list is either a list of parameters or a list of collections.

For the purpose of this investigation we used this framework to set build parameters which chose code variants or values in OpenACC clauses. The parameters targeted for the auto-tuning on each algorithm are the number of elements, *nel*; matrix size, N; scalar reduction, the number of OpenACC *gangs* and *workers* and the OpenACC *vector length*. An example of DSL script can be seen in Appendix.

4   Performance Results

The performance tests of the stand-alone benchmark and NekBone version with OpenACC have been carried out on a Cray XK6/XK7 system consisting of eighth compute nodes that comprises a 2.1 GHz AMD Interlagos 16-core processor, 16 GByte memory and one Kepler K20 NVIDIA Tesla GPU with 5 GByte of memory. Version 8.1 of the Cray Compilation Environment(CCE) supporting Open-ACC was used and the computational performance is measured in Gflops.

4.1   Benchmark

We first tested the performance of our stand-alone benchmark based on the number of elements. It is expected that the performance characteristics for the GPU will vary significantly with *nel*. In Fig. 2 we present the results for cases 1 and 2 running a *default* version of the kernels, i.e. the simplest OpenACC accelerated kernel which would let the compiler to take optimization decisions.

The performance of the *auto-tuned* version for cases 1 and 2 is also shown in Fig. 3. The performance results of case 3 are not shown due to they are very similar to case 2. The performance results obtained from auto-tuning show significant improvements over the *default* option in all situations. Furthermore, there is very little difference between the auto-tuned performance for case 1, 2 and 3.

4.2   Nekbone

Our main goal is to investigate what effect the kernel auto-tuning has on overall Nekbone performance. Therefore, after obtaining the optimal parameter settings from auto-tuning our stand-alone benchmark, they are now introduced into an OpenACC accelerated version of Nekbone. As useful reference values we have

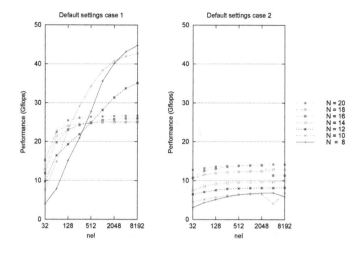

Fig. 2. Default performance of cases 1 (left) and 2 (right)

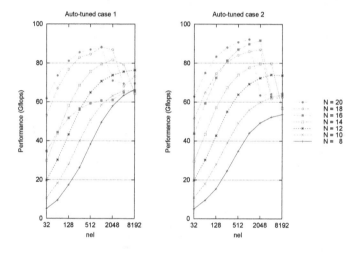

Fig. 3. Auto-tuned performance of cases 1 (left) and 2 (right)

used the previous performance results obtained by Markidis et al. using an accelerated OpenACC hand-tuned version of Nekbone. This performance result of a hand-tuned version can be seen on Fig. 4 (left). The maximum value of *nel* is often smaller than the previous value of 81292 used in the kernel benchmarks and the reason is that Nekbone uses more memory, and the application run into memory limits on the GPU (generally at large N).

To illustrate the effect of parameter tuning, Fig. 4 (right) shows the performance results of an auto-tuned version of Nekbone. This performance results demonstrates that auto-tuning technologies can be able to achieve similar or even improved performance results over hand-tuned codes. In Fig. 5 we have represented

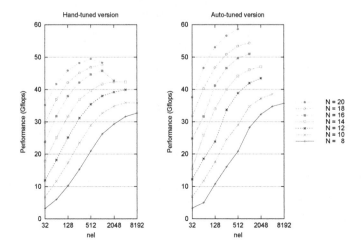

Fig. 4. Performance of a hand-tuned (left) by Markidis et al. and an auto-tuned (right) OpenACC Nekbone

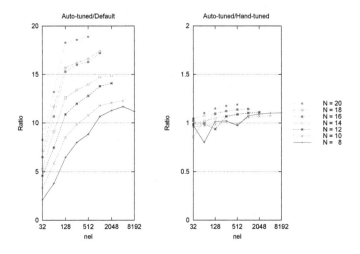

Fig. 5. Performance ratio of auto-tuned, hand-tuned and default OpenACC settings

the ratio between of our auto-tuned performance results over the hand-tuned performance results achieved by Markidis et al. and and using default OpenACC settings. It can be seen in Fig. 5 (right) that in some occasions the auto-tuned optimized version of Nekbone has achieved up to 20 % of performance improvement over the hand-tuned version. Note the difference in scale between the graphs shown in Fig. 5.

Thanks to the new Nekbone structure developed for this purpose and the exhaustive exploration of different parameter values carried out by the auto-tuner we have accomplished a simpler, better structured and faster implementation of

Nekbone. Furthermore, the exploration of different OpenACC optimization algorithms has revealed that loop collapsing techniques have given the best performance improvement among all the other techniques listed in Sect. 3. Although scalar reduction showed little performance improvement, the best performance vector-length values were 128 and 256.

5   Conclusions

The focus of this work was on accelerating Nek5000 using OpenACC compiler directives and auto-tuning technologies. Due to the complexity of Nek5000, our experiments have been carried out on a simplified version of the Nek5000 code, called Nekbone; and an extracted computational benchmark also based on Nek5000. A naive implementation using OpenACC showed little performance compared to an auto-tuned implementation where performance improvements of over 2x have been achieved. In addition, we have developed an OpenACC accelerated auto-tuned version of Nekbone. In this paper we have demonstrated that our auto-tuned version was able to reach, and some occasions improve, the performance accomplish by an OpenACC hand-tuned version.

A   Example of DSL Script

```
begin configuration
 begin tune
  mode: scenarios
  scenario-params: ALG
  scope: VECTOR_LENGTH N NEL NUM_GANGS VECTOR_LENGTH
  target: max
  metric-source: file
  postrun-metric-file: Output/output.$run_id
  metric-placement: lastregexp
  metric-regexp: tune run metric +(\S+)
 end tune
end configuration

begin parameters
 begin typing
  label NUM_GANGS
  label NUM_WORKERS
  int VECTOR_LENGTH
  int N
  int NEL
  int ALG
 end typing
 begin constraints
  range NUM_GANGS none default none
  range NUM_WORKERS none 1 2 4 8 16 32 default none
  range VECTOR_LENGTH 128 256 512 1024 default 128
  range ALG 101 102 103 104 105 106 107 108 109 110 default 101
  range N 8 10 12 14 16 18 20 default 8
```

```
  range NEL 32 64 128 512 1024 2048 4096 8192 default 32
!  runtime parameters first in this list
  depends NUM_WORKERS VECTOR_LENGTH N NEL
 end constraints
 !anything changed here, need to re-compile
 begin collections
  BUILD: NUM_WORKERS VECTOR_LENGTH
  end collections
 end parameters

 begin build
  command: cp sizes/mysize.$N.$NEL SIZE; ./makenek xx $NUM_WORKERS $VECTOR_LENGTH
  end build

 begin run
  command: aprun -n1 -N1 ./nekproxy $ALG > Output/output.$run_id
 end run
```

References

1. Egri, G., Fodor, Z., Hoelbling, C., Katz, S., Nogradi, D., Szabo, K.: Lattice QCD as a video game. Comput. Phys. Commun. **177**, 631–639 (2007)
2. Yasuda, K.: J. Comput. Chem. **29**, 334 (2007)
3. Fung, W.W.L., Aamodt, T.M.: Energy efficient GPU transactional memory via space-time optimizations. ACM, MICRO-46, pp. 408–420 (2013)
4. Nivia Tesla architecture (2014). http://www.nvidia.com/object/tesla-supercomputing-solutions.html. Accesed 14 January 2014
5. The CUDA Toolkit (2014). https://developer.nvidia.com/cuda-downloads. Accesed 14 January 2014
6. Coleman, D.M., Feldman, D.R.: Porting existing radiation code for GPU acceleration. IEEE J. Sel. Top. Appl. Earth Obs. Remote Sens. **6**(6), 1–6 (2013)
7. Delgado, J., Gazolla, J., Clua, E., Masoud Sadjadi, S.: A case study on porting scientific applications to GPU/CUDA. J. Comput. Interdisc. Sci. **2**(1), 3–11 (2011)
8. OpenMP 4.0 (2014). http://openmp.org/wp/. Accessed 14 January 2014
9. OpenACC. OpenACC Home Page (2014). http://openacc.org/. Accessed 14 January 2014
10. Hoshino, T., Maruyama, N., Matsuoka, S., Takaki, R.: CUDA vs OpenACC: performance case studies with kernel benchmarks and a memory-bound CFD application. In: IEEE International Symposium on Cluster Computing and the Grid, pp. 136–143 (2013)
11. Gray, A., Hart, A., Richardson, A., Stratford, K.: Lattice boltzmann for large-scale gpu systems. In: PARCO, pp. 167–174 (2011)
12. Chen, J.H., Choudhary, A., De Supinski, B., DeVries, M., Hawkes, E., Klasky, S., Liao, W., Ma, K., Mellor-Crummey, J., Podhorszki, N., et al.: Terascale direct numerical simulations of turbulent combustion using s3d. Comput. Sci. Discov. **2**, 1 (2009)
13. Fischer, P., Heisey, K., Kruse, J., Mullen, J., Tufo, H., Lottes, J.: Nek5000 Premier (2014). http://www.csc.cs.colorado.edu/voran/nek/nekdoc/primer.pdf. Accessed 10 January 2014

14. Fischer, P., Heisey, K.: NEKBONE: Thermal Hydraulics mini-application. Nekbone Release 2.1 (2013). https://cesar.mcs.anl.gov/content/software/thermal_hydraulics. Accessed 10 January 2014
15. Markidis, S., Gong, J., Schliephake, M., Laure E., Hart, A., Henty, D., Heisey, P., Fischer, P.: OpenACC Acceleration of Nek5000, Spectral Element Code
16. Shin, J., Hall, M.W., Chame, J., Chen, C., Fischer, P.F., Hovland, P.D.: Speeding up Nek5000 with autotuning and specialization. In: Proceedings of the 24th ACM International Conference on Supercomputing, pp. 253–262 (2010)
17. Patera, A.T.: A spectral element method for uid dynamics: laminar flow in a channel expansion. J. Comput. Phys. **54**(3), 468–488 (1984)
18. Dongarra, J.J., Du Croz, J., Duff, I.S., Hammarling, S.: Algorithm 679: a set of level 3 basic linear algebra subprograms. ACM Trans. Math. Soft. **16**, 18–28 (1990)
19. IBM Compilers (2014). http://www-03.ibm.com/software/products/en/sub category/SW780. Accessed 15 January 2014
20. Intel Compilers (2014). http://software.intel.com/en-us/intel-compilers. Accessed 15 January 2014
21. The Portland Group (PGI). http://www.pgroup.com/. Accessed 15 January 2014
22. The GNU Compiler Collection. http://gcc.gnu.org. Accessed 15 January 2014
23. Richardson, H.: Domain specific language (DSL) for expressing parallel auto-tuning, CRESTA Project Deliverable D3.6.2 (2014). http://cresta-project.eu/table/deliverables/year-1-deliverables/. Accessed 16 January 2014
24. Anderson, J.: Modern Compressible Flow: With Historical Perspective. McGraw-Hill, New York (2003)
25. CRESTA Research Project (2014). http://cresta-project.eu/. Accessed 20 March 2014

Development Environment
for Exascale Applications

Towards Exascale Co-design in a Runtime System

Thomas Sterling, Matthew Anderson[(✉)], P. Kevin Bohan, Maciej Brodowicz, Abhishek Kulkarni, and Bo Zhang

Center for Research in Extreme Scale Technologies,
School of Informatics and Computing, Indiana University,
Bloomington, IN, USA
andersmw@indiana.edu

Abstract. Achieving the performance potential of an Exascale machine depends on realizing both operational efficiency and scalability in high performance computing applications. This requirement has motivated the emergence of several new programming models which emphasize fine and medium grain task parallelism in order to address the aggravating effects of asynchrony at scale. The performance modeling of Exascale systems for these programming models requires the development of fundamentally new approaches due to the demands of both scale and complexity. This work presents a performance modeling case study of the Livermore Unstructured Lagrangian Explicit Shock Hydrodynamics (LULESH) proxy application where the performance modeling approach has been incorporated directly into a runtime system with two modalities of operation: computation and performance modeling simulation. The runtime system exposes performance sensitivies and projects operation to larger scales while also realizing the benefits of removing global barriers and extracting more parallelism from LULESH. Comparisons between the computation and performance modeling simulation results are presented.

1 Introduction

Understanding and managing asynchrony effects in simulating Exascale parallel machines with eventual billion-way parallelism is a crucial factor in achieving application efficiency and scalability. Efforts to manage asynchrony have resulted in the creation of a number of emerging programming models and the renovation of several traditional programming models all with the aim to utilize asynchrony and extract more parallelism from applications at large scale. A key component of these efforts is performance modeling.

Several performance models have been created specifically to highlight shortcomings in how traditional programming models fail to adequately address asynchrony. One of these is the Starvation-Latency-Overhead-Waiting for Contention (SLOW) performance model [14] where each letter of the acronym SLOW identifies one of the key causes for constrained scalability in an application and

© Springer International Publishing Switzerland 2015
S. Markidis and E. Laure (Eds.): EASC 2014, LNCS 8759, pp. 85–99, 2015.
DOI: 10.1007/978-3-319-15976-8_6

highlights a challenge when programming using the conventional practice. Several alternatives to conventional practice have been developed to better address the issues highlighted by SLOW by utilitizing lightweight concurrent threads managed using synchronization primitives such as dataflow and futures in order to alter the application flow structure from being message-passing to becoming message-driven.

However, the performance modeling necessary to understand and manage asynchrony effects at scale can be especially challenging for emerging programming models that rely on lightweight concurrent threads. Trace-driven approaches for such programming models tend to substantially alter the application execution path itself while cycle-accurate simulations tend to be too expensive for co-design efforts. While discrete event simulators have been successfully used for the performance modeling of many-tasking execution models before [4], they require both an implementation of the execution model in the simulator as well as a skeleton application implementation. This skeleton code has to preserve the dataflow of the original application while appropriately modeling the computational costs of the full application in between communication requests.

A robust implementation of the execution model in the discrete event simulator and a close representation between the skeleton code and the full application are both crucial in order to achieve accurate performance predictions from the discrete event simulator. A skeleton code which closely represents the computational costs and dataflow of the full application code can be especially difficult to achieve because a significant code fork is necessary in order to develop the skeleton code. Updates and improvements made to the full application code are not automatically reflected in the skeleton code and inconsistencies between the two codes are easily introduced. Likewise, accuracy in implementing the execution model in the event simulator is also difficult to achieve: modeling the contention on resources, the variable overheads when using concurrent threads, the highly variable communication incidence rates, the network latency hiding, the thread schedulers and associated contention, and the oversubscription behavior all contribute in complicating the implementation of the execution model in the discrete event simulator.

This paper presents a performance modeling case study for many-tasking execution models which incorporates performance modeling directly into the runtime system implementation of the execution model without requiring a skeleton code or application traces. A runtime system is the best equipped tool for performance modeling an application as it comes with the necessary introspection capability, it does not require a skeleton code separate from the application for modeling, and is itself already a robust implementation of the execution model it represents. For this case study, the performance modeling capability of the HPX-5 runtime system is explored for a proxy application developed by one of the US Department of Energy co-design centers: the Livermore Unstructured Lagrangian Explicit Shock Hydrodynamics (LULESH) proxy application code [1]. LULESH has been ported to multiple programming models, both emerging and traditional, and its scaling behavior has been extensively explored making it a good candidate for this case study. More importantly, the scientific kernel encapsulated in the LULESH proxy application is expected to be representative of computational science applications requiring future Exascale resources.

The HPX-5 runtime system is an implementation of the ParalleX execution model [9] and supports message-driven computation as well as two different modalities of operation: full computation and performance modeling simulation, hereafter referred to as simulation. The simulation modality in this case study is restricted to those cases where the prototype Exascale node is already available for simulation. This enables the runtime system to produce performance predictions for large systems composed of those prototype nodes. This approach that does not require a separate skeleton code nor code tracing instrumentation for use in performance studies and application co-design.

Overall, this work provides the following new contributions:

- It presents a port of LULESH proxy application to the ParalleX execution model.
- It presents a performance modeling approach for many-tasking execution models where the performance modeling has been incorporated into the runtime system.
- It presents a performance modeling approach that is not trace-driven and does not require a skeleton code.
- It explores a runtime system with two modalities of operation for both performance modeling simulation and full computation operation.

This work is structured as follows. Related work is given in Sect. 2, followed by a description of the performance modeling approach proposed here. Details about the runtime system used in the case study are given in Sect. 4 along with motivation why modern runtime systems are well suited for performance modeling when using a many-tasking execution model. Secton 5 gives details about the HPX-5 implementation of LULESH used here while Sect. 6 presents the results of the LULESH case study. Our conclusions and directions for future work are given in Sect. 7.

2   Related Work

While there have been a large number of approaches to developing performance modeling techniques which are application independent, most of these have centered around the Communicating Sequential Processes (CSP) execution model. Trace-driven approaches are a key component in many performance modeling and co-design frameworks, including DUMPI in SST/Macro [11], Log-GOPSim [10], and the Performance Modeling and Characterization (PMaC) framework [6]. A key challenge in trace-driven approaches is the trace collection overhead. Carrington et al. [5] demonstrate how to reduce the trace collection overhead by extrapolating results to larger core count sizes using smaller core count traces. While trace-based approaches generally do not require changes to the user application and work well with the coarse-grained computation style favored by CSP, trace collection overhead can significantly alter the execution path for the fine-grained computation style favored in many-tasking execution models.

A domain specific language (DSL) approach to performance modeling was introduced by Spafford et al. [13], named Aspen. Aspen provides a common set of tools and concepts to more easily enable coarse-grained exploration of algorithms and co-design. However, Aspen also makes some limiting assumptions which could prevent fine-grained, message-driven style computations. To work around such shortcomings, the message-driven toolkit Charm++provides its own trace-driven parallel discrete event simulator, BigSim [15], which is itself capable of parallel computation. When used in conjunction with the Charm++performance emulator, BigSim Emulator [16], coarse timing predictions can be made to guide co-design decisions. As it is a trace-driven approach, the traces can impact the execution path of sufficiently fine-grained computations.

In the context of fine-grained computations with significant resource oversub-scription, performance modeling options for many-tasking execution models are very few and, up to now, require skeleton code creation in order to avoid trace-driven approaches. Sottile et al. [12] present a semi-automatic way of extracting software skeletons using source-to-source code generation as one way to avoid forking application codes for discrete event simulation. Robust, generic, and fully automatic approaches for skeleton code generation are difficult to find.

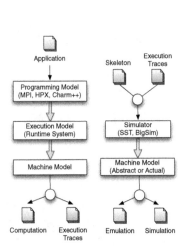

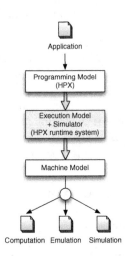

(a) Traditional simulation approaches are either trace-driven or skeleton code driven making the application one step removed from the simulator.

(b) An alternative approach takes advantage of the increasing runtime system introspection available to add simulation capability directly to the runtime.

Fig. 1. An illustration comparing the traditional performance modeling approaches with what is proposed here.

3   Performance Modeling

This case study targets performance modeling scenarios where the actual or prototype Exascale node is available. Unlike traditional simulation approaches, the proposed simulation methodology does not involve generating traces nor a skeleton code but rather integrating the simulation capability with the runtime system. Figure 1 highlights the differences between traditional simulation approaches and what is proposed here. This alternative approach is motivated by the goal of improving user access to performance modeling, the rapid increase in the number of many-tasking execution models, and the ability for modern runtime systems to incorporate all necessary introspection mechanisms to properly operate in a performance modeling simulation mode. Further motivation as to why the runtime system is well suited for this type of modeling is provided in Sect. 4.

For any application, the many-tasking runtime system has full and direct access to the task phase information. When the runtime is operating in a simulation modality on prototype Exascale nodes, a sample of nodes is selected for performing the application simulation. Other nodes that directly interact with these nodes are also simulated but only for a small set of communication iterations to provide accurate message incidence rates for the sample nodes. Using select iteration snapshots in the course of the application simulation, the runtime system uses these sample nodes to predict application performance at the scale indicated by the user. While this approach does not require traces, it has a disadvantage of not providing performance predictions for the entire duration of application execution. The performance predictions are provided only for a specific subset of communication iterations.

The approach is illustrated in Fig. 2. Each square and circle represents a node in an Exascale simulation while arrows indicate communication. When the runtime system is in simulation mode, a user defined set of sample nodes, indicated by the red outlined boxes, is selected for running the application. Nodes which interact with this sample set, indicated by blue circles, are identified by the runtime system accessing the node interaction data. The application is also run on these nodes in order to provide correct incidence rates and phase information to the sample nodes but their runtime information, such as specific execution times of various subroutines, is not used in the performance prediction. Network communication is performed between all nodes that are running the application while a network model handles communication between circle nodes and non-running ghost nodes, indicated by blue squares. Green arrows indicate network traffic approximated by a network model, red arrows indicate real network traffic, and black arrows indicate traffic not modeled.

The accuracy of the predictions relies on how well the sample nodes represent the overall state of the application. For static dataflow applications which are well-balanced, this would be easily achieved with a very small sample size. For highly dynamic applications, it would not be unlikely to require terascale computing in order to predict Exascale performance.

This runtime system based approach can be improved and refined in several ways. The number of buffer nodes which provide incidence rate and node interaction information to the sample set can be increased to improve accuracy. Likewise, the introspection capability of the runtime system can be expanded to directly model these phases and incidence rates while in full computation mode and then later re-used in the simulation modality while still avoiding trace collection. In this case study, we present results from the simplest performance modeling approach where sample nodes operate in full computation mode with all other nodes operating as ghost (non-computing) nodes. The following section gives details about the runtime system selected for this case study and how runtime system capabilites are well suited for taking on the role of performance modeling.

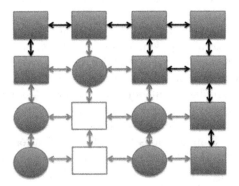

Fig. 2. A runtime system based performance modeling approach. Each square and circle represents a node in an Exascale simulation while arrows indicate communication. When the runtime system is in simulation mode, a user defined set of sample nodes, indicated by the red outlined boxes, is selected for running the application. Nodes which interact with this sample set, indicated by blue circles, are identified by the runtime system accessing the node interaction data. The application is also run on these nodes in order to provide correct incidence rates and phase information to the sample nodes but their runtime information is not used in the performance prediction. Network communication is performed between all nodes that are running the application while a network model handles communication between circle nodes and non-running ghost nodes, indicated by blue squares. Green arrows indicate network traffic modeled by a network model, red arrows indicate real network traffic, and black arrows indicate traffic not modeled.

4   Runtime Systems and Performance Modeling

Performance modeling of Exascale systems requires development of fundamentally new approaches due to demands of both scale and complexity. The trace based methodologies are infamous for generating prohibitively large volumes of data when run on many nodes of a large system, necessitating the use of the on-the-fly compression that potentially distorts timing, or decimation of data, which reduces overall accuracy. Full scale fine-grain discrete event simulation may easily exceed the application's run time on the actual hardware. The skeleton based approximations may result in faster simulation, but also tend to reduce the accuracy due to overly simplified models of execution resources, memory, and network, as well as their interactions. To address these shortcomings, an approach inspired by and integrated with the model of execution is proposed. Unlike most existing solutions that necessarily restrict their functionality to a single or at most a few layers of system software stack, execution model spans the whole gamut of software services and underlying hardware, permitting more thorough analysis. The ParalleX execution model and its associated HPX-5 runtime system implementation are used for this case study.

ParalleX is a new model of execution explicitly created to identify and mitigate the effects of primary sources of performance degradation in parallel applications. They include: (i) **S**tarvation, or insufficient amount of work necessary to efficiently utilize the available execution resources, (ii) **L**atency, or delay in accessing remote resources and services, (iii) **O**verhead, or additional work required for management of parallel computations and resource allocation on critical path, but absent from the sequential variant, and (iv) **W**aiting for resolution of contention on concurrently accessed resources and services. The newly added extensions of the ParalleX model deal with **E**nergy efficiency of computation and its **R**esilience, or achieving reliable execution in the presence of faults (SLOWER). ParalleX addresses many limitations of commonly used application programming models such as MPI, by breaking free of Communicating Sequential Processes scheme (which frequently results in overly constrained implementations abusing global barriers). Instead ParalleX relies on message-driven approach that avoids predetermined patterns of interaction by combining lightweight threads, fine-grain synchronization, and active messages called *parcels*.

Even though some of the model components have been known for more than a decade, ParalleX organizes them into a novel parallel execution framework with unified semantics. The system is subdivided into a number of localities, or physical resources with bounded service response time. In typical platforms (clusters, constellations), locality corresponds to a computational node. The localities are connected by asynchronously operating network. Application state may be arbitrarily distributed across any number of localities in the system. Local modifications of application state are carried out by threads. In ParalleX, threads are by definition ephemeral, created for and existing only long enough to execute a specific task. This makes them a convenient medium to represent the unconstrained parallelism available in the application. Thread execution is synchronized by Local Control Objects (LCOs). These structures implement high-level synchronization primitives, such as futures or dataflow elements, although support of traditional atomic operations is also possible. Both threads and LCOs are closely integrated with scheduling algorithms to permit event-driven operation (and avoiding busy-waits and polling) as much as possible.

Threads and LCOs along with related data structures can be embedded in ParalleX processes — entities that hierarchically organize parallel computation and provide logical encapsulation for its individual components. Unlike UNIX processes, they can span multiple localities (and therefore multiple address spaces). Processes, threads, and LCOs may migrate between the nodes and are globally addressable, permitting the programmer to access them from anywhere in the system. This is controlled by the Active Global Address Space (AGAS), a distributed service that maintains lookup tables storing physical locations of all first class objects of the computation. ParalleX functionality manifests itself primarily in the runtime system layer, which, through its proximity to the application code permits additional optimizations and acts as an intermediate layer for access to expensive (in terms of overhead and latency) OS kernel services. ParalleX compliant runtime system implements introspection, supporting direct access to integrated performance counters and enabling monitoring of application activity. This is particularly valuable for low overhead collection of performance data.

HPX-5 is a high performance runtime system that implements the ParalleX model, providing the ability to run HPC applications at-scale and to simulate the performance characteristics of code without actually fully running the application.

Written in C and assembly, the HPX-5 runtime system is focused primarily on algorithmic correctness, performance, and stability. To achieve this, HPX-5 is developed with an extensive suite of tests that execute well known scientific codes with published results and uses these to ensure correctness and stability.

The runtime is highly modular and is comprised of several components, including:

- A user-space *thread manager* made up of M:N coroutines similar to Python Green Threads. HPX-5 threads are continously rebalanced across logical CPU cores in a NUMA-aware way that ensures a high degree of continuous work.
- An asynchronous network layer built on RDMA *verbs* capable of running on InfiniBand, Cray Gemini, and Ethernet networks as well as in a non-networked (SMP) environment.
- A *parcel dispatch* system that routes messages between objects and makes runtime optimizations through direct integration with the node's network interface controller (NIC).
- A variety of distributed lock-free control structures, including *futures* and logical gates that provide programmers with an easy-to-use environment in which to define application dataflow.
- An *active global address space* (AGAS) that automatically distributes and balances data across all nodes in an HPC system.
- Support for multi-core embedded architectures (such as ARM).
- Instrumentation to perform simulations of application runs in a variety of environments, using *spec files* that describe several well-known machines.

In addition to normal operation, the HPX-5 runtime supports a *simulation* mode in which it models performance of a full (non-skeleton) computation application as it would run on a target system. It achieves this in two ways: a) by directly modeling performance on the target system (simulation), and b) by emulating the performance of system other than the one it is running on through the use of pre-generated specification files that detail the typical performance characteristics of the target system's hardware as well as interconnect network topology and other features.

Using the ParalleX execution model, the MPI based LULESH proxy application has been ported to the HPX-5 runtime system. The following section briefly describes this port and how it differs from the MPI implementation.

5   ParalleX LULESH

The implementation of LULESH in ParalleX is optimized by removing global barrier calls like `Allreduce` and overlapping the communcation needed for the reduction operation with computation. Owing to this, ParalleX is able to extract some performance benefits over the original MPI implementation of LULESH. The HPX-5 implementation of the LULESH application is based on the same domain-element hierarchy employed in the MPI version available at [2]. But it differs from the MPI implementation in three aspects.

First, the two implementations differ in how they determine the time increment. Specifically, at the end of each iteration, each element computes a time increment satisfying the local Courant and Hydro constraints and the minimum value among all elements is used as the next time step. In the MPI-implementation, this is done by placing a blocking collective `MPI_Allreduce` at the beginning of each iteration (see Fig. 3a). In contrast, the HPX-5 implementation replaces the `MPI_Allreduce` call with a nonblocking `future` and does not wait for its completion until after completing `ApplyAccelerationBoundary Condition`, where the time increment is first needed (see Fig. 3b). As a result, the HPX-5 implementation can effectively overlap the communication and computation phases associated with the reduction operation.

The second difference between the two versions is oversubscription. In the MPI-implementation, each core on a compute node is responsible for one domain. For the HPX-5 implementation, it is normal to assign more than one domain to one core. Oversubscription in conjunction with nonblocking synchronization semantics enable computation to overlap with communication effectively hiding network latency.

Lastly, each domain has three fixed communication patterns in the course of the computation in the HPX-5 implementation. The MPI-implementation regenerates the communication pattern with neighboring domains each time communication occurs even though it is always the same.

These changes have an immediate and visible impact on the computational phases of LULESH. Figure 4 compares the computational phases between MPI LULESH and HPX-5 LULESH on 64 processors where red indicates computation and white indicates communication. By replacing global barriers with futures based nonblocking communication, the time spent waiting for communication to complete can be reduced substantially in an application.

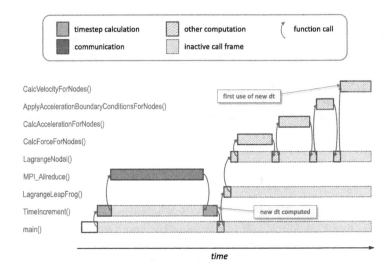

(a) Call sequence determining the global time step value along with the follow-on computations in the original MPI LULESH code. The new time step is returned by the allreduce operation which blocks until all contributing processes reach the same execution point, effectively imposing a barrier. Even though several functions could start execution (their workload does not depend on the new time step value), they are blocked until the communication phase completes.

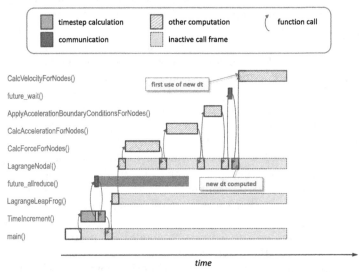

(b) Call sequence of the HPX-5 LULESH version of the code shown above using future for a non-blocking collective operation. After **future_allreduce** returns, the pending computations that do not depend on the new time step may proceed immediately, overlapping the communication phase. A portion of the code from **TimeIncrement** function has to be moved after **future_wait** to correctly post-process the new time step value. The combined latency of **future_allreduce** and **future_wait** calls is usually substantially shorter than that of blocking allreduce on a large machine.

Fig. 3.

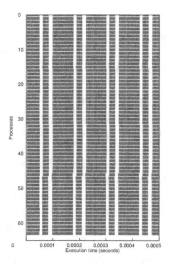

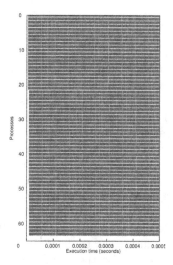

(a) The computational phases for MPI LULESH on 64 processors. Red indicates computation while white indicates waiting for communication.

(b) The computational phases for HPX LULESH on 64 processors. Red indicates computation while white indicates waiting for communication.

Fig. 4. A comparison of computational phases between MPI and HPX versions of LULESH.

6 Results

Strong and weak scaling results for HPX-5 LULESH are presented in this section along with the runtime system's performance predictions. All computations and simulations were performed on 16-node Xeon E5-2670 2.60 GHz based cluster with an Infiniband interconnect. The oversubscription factor for all distributed cases was two; that is, the entire LULESH computational domain was partitioned into twice as many subdomains as available cores.

Our simulation approach is most similar to SMPI [7] where online simulation (or emulation) is performed on a subset of the nodes. The rest of the nodes in the simulation are either ignored or simulated depending on the application requirements. In case of LULESH, we computed the global values offline such that there were no message dependencies from the simulated nodes to the emulated nodes. For structured communication patterns, we use periodic boundary conditions to meet the receive depenences from the simulated nodes to the emulated nodes. Since the pending receives can generate load on the emulated nodes, we are presently working on recovering these dependences through offline traces. Communication is performed only between emulated nodes. For network simulation, we used the LogP cost model [8] to calculate communication time for the simulated nodes. Under the assumption that each parcel is sent using a single message[1], per the LogGP [3] model, a send was computed to take $(2 \times o) + (n-1)G + L$ cycles where L is the network latency, o is the overhead of transmission and G is the gap per byte. The LoGP parameters for the 16-node Xeon E5-2670 2.60 GHz based cluster were measured empirically for the above experiments.

In Fig. 5, the workload was increased from 1 to 512 domains as the number of nodes were increased from 1 to 16. The simulator introduces some overhead since it has to inspect every message and either emulate or simulate it. We found that the predicted value was within 25 % of the actual running time. The strong-scaling results in Fig. 6 confirm the above observation. For the above runs, each "simulated" workload was run with half the number of actual nodes. Figure 7 shows the simulation accuracy of our online simulation approach. We see that the accuracy improves (that is, the difference between the emulated and simulated value decreases) as the number of emulated nodes are increased. This confirms the trade-off between simulation accuracy and the computation requirements for the simulation. As stated previously, simulating the performance of the application at Exascale levels might demand considerable computation resources. Hence, such an approach where the accuracy can be bounded by sampling a subset of the available nodes might be favorable.

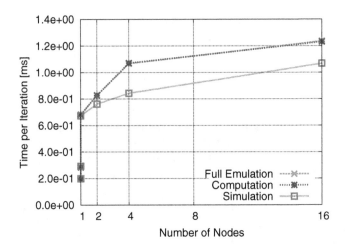

Fig. 5. Weak scaling results for HPX-5 LULESH. "Computation" represents the actual running time for a fixed workload for 500 iterations. "Full Emulation" indicates the time to perform full emulation of the workload using our hybrid emulation and simulation approach. "Simulation" shows the running time predicted by the simulator.

---

[1] Almost all messages were under 32K for our HPX-5 port of the LULESH application.

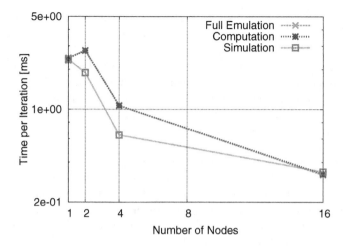

Fig. 6. Strong scaling performance of HPX-5 LULESH across 16 nodes. The description of the legend is same as the previous figure, Fig. 5.

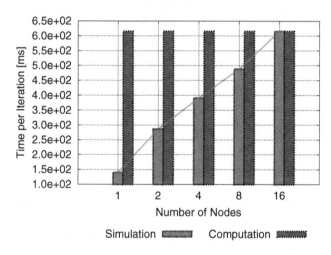

Fig. 7. Simulation accuracy as the number of emulated nodes are increased. A prediction is more accurate if the difference between the computation and simulation times is lower.

7   Conclusions

Efficiency and scalability requirements for high performance computing applications has cultivated the development of new programming models which employ fine and medium grain task parallelism creating challenges for performance modeling at Exascale. In particular, task-driven approaches cause significant problems for runtime systems using lightweight concurrent threads while discrete event simulators require skeleton codes which are difficult to reliably extract from the full application codes. At the same time, runtime systems now regularly provide the introspection capability to reliably carry out performance modeling within the runtime system itself. An approach to incorporating performance modeling in the runtime system has been described here for use in cases where a prototype Exascale node is available for computation. Using a sampling approach in conjunction with a network model, a runtime system can be quickly transformed into a performance modeling tool without requiring traces nor discrete event simulation.

A case study has also been presented here where the LULESH proxy application has been ported to the HPX-5 runtime system and run in both of the computation and simulation modalities provided by the runtime. The HPX-5 LULESH port illustrates all of the features of a many-tasking implementation, including oversubscription, asynchrony management semantics, and active messages. Strong and weak scaling results were provided for comparison between the computation and simulation modalities.

Incorporating performance modeling into modern runtime systems resolves several issues when operating at Exascale while also simplifying co-design for application developers. While such an approach is new and mostly untested, it ultimately can remove one layer of separation between application development and performance modeling for approaches employing fine and medium grain task parallelism.

Acknowledgments. The authors acknowledge Benjamin Martin, Jackson DeBuhr, Ezra Kissel, Luke D'Alessandro, and Martin Swany for their technical assistance.

References

1. Hydrodynamics Challenge Problem, Lawrence Livermore National Laboratory. Technical Report LLNL-TR-490254
2. Livermore unstructured lagrangian explicit shock hydrodynamics (lulesh). https://codesign.llnl.gov/lulesh.php
3. Alexandrov, A., Ionescu, M.F., Schauser, K.E., Scheiman, C.: LogGP: incorporating long messages into the LogP modelone step closer towards a realistic model for parallel computation. In: Proceedings of the Seventh Annual ACM Symposium on Parallel Algorithms and Architectures, SPAA 1995, pp. 95–105. ACM, New York, NY, USA (1995)
4. Anderson, M., Brodowicz, M., Kulkarni, A., Sterling, T.: Performance modeling of gyrokinetic toroidal simulations for amany-tasking runtime system. In: Jarvis, S.A., Wright, S.A., Hammond, S.D. (eds.) High Performance Computing Systems. Performance Modeling, Benchmarking and Simulation. LNCS, pp. 136–157. Springer, Heidelberg (2014)
5. Carrington, L., Laurenzano, M., Tiwari, A.: Inferring large-scale computation behavior via trace extrapolation. In: Large-Scale Parallel Processing workshop (IPDPS 2013)
6. Carrington, L., Snavely, A., Gao, X., Wolter, N.: A performance prediction framework for scientific applications. In: ICCS Workshop on Performance Modeling and Analysis (PMA03), pp. 926–935 (2003)

7. Clauss, P.-N., Stillwell, M., Genaud, S., Suter, F., Casanova, H., Quinson, M.: Single node on-line simulation of MPI applications with SMPI. In: Parallel Distributed Processing Symposium (IPDPS), 2011 IEEE International, pp. 664–675 (2011)
8. Culler, D., Karp, R., Patterson, D., Sahay, A., Schauser, K.E., Santos, E., Subramonian, R., von Eicken, T.: LogP: towards a realistic model of parallel computation. In: Proceedings of the Fourth ACM SIGPLAN Symposium on Principles and Practice Of Parallel Programming, PPOPP 1993, pp. 1–12. ACM, New York, NY, USA (1993)
9. Gao, G., Sterling, T., Stevens, R., Hereld, M., Zhu, W.: ParalleX: a study of a new parallel computation model. In: Parallel and Distributed Processing Symposium. IPDPS 2007. IEEE International, pp. 1–6 (2007)
10. Hoefler, T., Schneider, T., Lumsdaine, A.: LogGOPSim - simulating large-scale applications in the LogGOPS Model. In: Proceedings of the 19th ACM International Symposium on High Performance Distributed Computing, pp. 597–604. ACM, June 2010
11. Janssen, C.L., Adalsteinsson, H., Cranford, S., Kenny, J.P., Pinar, A., Evensky, D.A., Mayo, J.: A simulator for large-scale parallel computer architectures. IJDST 1(2), 57–73 (2010)
12. Sottile, M., Dakshinamurthy, A., Hendry, G., Dechev, D.: Semi-automatic extraction of software skeletons for benchmarking large-scale parallel applications. In: Proceedings of the 2013 ACM SIGSIM Conference on Principles of Advanced Discrete Simulation, SIGSIM-PADS 2013, pp. 1–10. ACM, New York, NY, USA (2013)
13. Spafford, K.L., Vetter, J.S.: Aspen: a domain specific language for performance modeling. In: Proceedings of the International Conference on High Performance Computing, Networking, Storage and Analysis, SC 2012, pp. 84:1–84:11. IEEE Computer Society Press, Los Alamitos, CA, USA (2012)
14. Sterling, T.: Towards a ParalleX-enabled Exascale Architecture. Presentation to the DOE Architecture 2 Workshop, 10 August 2011
15. Totoni, E., Bhatele, A., Bohm, E., Jain, N., Mendes, C., Mokos, R., Zheng, G., Kale, L.: Simulation-based performance analysis and tuning for a two-level directly connected system. In: Proceedings of the 17th IEEE International Conference on Parallel and Distributed Systems, December 2011
16. Zheng, G., Wilmarth, T., Lawlor, O.S., Kalé, L.V., Adve, S., Padua, D., Geubelle, P.: Performance modeling and programming environments for Petaflops computers and the Blue Gene machine. In: NSF Next Generation Systems Program Workshop, 18th International Parallel and Distributed Processing Symposium(IPDPS), p. 197. IEEE Press, Santa Fe, New Mexico, April 2004

Overcoming Asynchrony: An Analysis of the Effects of Asynchronous Noise on Nearest Neighbor Synchronizations

Adam Hammouda[1][(✉)], Andrew Siegel[1], and Stephen Siegel[2]

[1] Argonne National Laboratory Mathematics and Computer Sciences Division, Lemont, IL 60439, USA
ahammouda@cs.uchicago.edu, siegela@mcs.anl.gov
http://cesar.mcs.anl.gov/
[2] University of Delaware Verified Software Laboratory, Newark, DE 19716, USA
siegel@udel.edu
http://vsl.cis.udel.edu

Abstract. A simple model of noise with an adjustable level of *asynchrony* is presented. The model is used to generate synthetic noise traces in the presence of a representative bulk synchronous, nearest neighbor time stepping algorithm. The resulting performance of the algorithm is measured and compared to the performance of the algorithm in the presence of Gaussian distributed noise. The results empirically illustrate that asynchrony is a dominant mechanism by which many types of computational noise degrade the performance of bulk-synchronous algorithms, whether or not their macroscopic noise distributions are constant or random.

Keywords: Performance analysis · Exascale · Noise · Stencil methods · Optimization · Fault tolerance · Resilience

1 Introduction

Understanding the sources and impact of computational noise on application performance is a growing concern for the HPC community [10]. Put simply, it is anticipated that next-generation HPC architectures will be characterized by inherent load imbalances arising from a broad range of noise sources. Details are discussed at length by Brown et al. [3], Snir et al. [10] and references therein. The net effect though is well understood – for applications, equal node work will not in general equate to equal execution time, and thus bulk synchronous algorithmic formulations will experience exceptional performance degradation.

This realization has forced us to re-examine research on both the sources of noise, and noise/algorithm interaction. While a number of related studies in this area (e.g. [1,2,4,6–8,11,12]) have advanced our understanding of computational noise, it is also safe to say that we have only begun to scratch the surface when

---

The rights of this work are transferred to the extent transferable according to title 17 §105 U.S.C.

© Springer International Publishing Switzerland 2015 (outside the US)
S. Markidis and E. Laure (Eds.): EASC 2014, LNCS 8759, pp. 100–109, 2015.
DOI: 10.1007/978-3-319-15976-8_7

it comes to understanding the full range of complexity of this problem. One case in point is the recent study by Beckman et al. [2] where the authors define and identify noise *asynchrony* as a key property in understanding how noise degrades application performance. Furthermore, they show that asynchronous noise has a much greater negative impact on the performance of global collective operations than synchronized noise.

We have observed similar phenomenon in previous work, in which a classic bulk-synchronous nearest neighbor time stepping algorithm was compared to a new, resilient formulation [5]. In this case, application runtime in the presence of Gaussian random noise was consistently underestimated by our predictions. We attributed this discrepancy to a failure to properly account for complex asynchronous-type properties characteristic of randomly distributed noise.

To our knowledge, no one has attempted to quantify asynchronous noise or its impact on the performance of bulk-synchronous codes. This realization has motivated our current study, where we present a simple quantitative model for asynchronous noise. Furthermore, we demonstrate that the mechanisms underlying asynchronous noise result in bounding behavior of the performance of bulk-synchronous algorithms in the presence of arbitrary and non-deterministic noise.

This work provides a valuable and necessary first step towards developing closed-form analytical models of the runtimes of general scientific computations in the presence of computational noise. Such work can provide valuable insight to hardware vendors and system software and middleware developers in designing the next generation hardware architectures and runtime environments. Moreover these insights themselves have intrinsic value at a time where computational noise is becoming an increasingly prominent and necessary evil on the path to exascale.

2   Characterization of Noise Profiles

In order to properly examine how the performance of bulk-synchronous computations are impacted by asynchronous noise, it is necessary to rigorously define

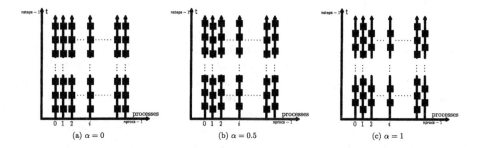

(a) $\alpha = 0$ (b) $\alpha = 0.5$ (c) $\alpha = 1$

Fig. 1. Figure Illustrating Physical Interpretation of α, asynchrony. α is simply the fraction by which neighboring process detours are offset from each other. The black squares represent detours and the lines through them represent the normal execution of an application on each process.

Table 1. Table of the Defining Variables of Noise.

Variable	Term	Definition
T	Detour duration	The length of time a process spends unable to perform the work of an application's code
π	Period	The period of time between every detour
α	Asynchrony	The term which governs the phase difference in periods between adjacent processes ($\alpha \in [0,1]$)
η	Lag	The lag before the first detour. It differs on each process according to Eq. (1)

what is meant by noise broadly, and then specifically what is meant by asynchronous noise.

As done in a previous study [5], we refer to each individual delay in an application's execution caused by an event external to the application itself as a *detour*. *Noise* then refers to the aggregate phenomena of every detour over some period of time.

If every detour occurs with a specified *period*, *asynchrony* can be thought of as the extent to which adjacent processes experience a phase difference between each other's periods. This in turn will affect the extent to which detours on neighboring processes overlap. Each processor experiences its first detour after a lag, η, defined by

$$
\eta \equiv \begin{cases} \pi & \text{if process is odd} \\ \pi + \alpha * T & \text{o/w.} \end{cases} \tag{1}
$$

Here, $0 \leq i \leq \mathsf{nprocs}-1$ and nprocs are the number of processes involved in a simulation. The full parameter space governing the manifestation of asynchronous noise is given in Table 1. For an illustration of asynchrony, see Fig. 1.

3   Experiments

We now examine the impact of asynchronous noise on bulk-synchronous algorithms. In order to simulate both constant frequency noise and Gaussian distributed noise, we utilize a set of noise generation utilities, developed initially for previous work [5], documentation of which can be found with its source code online [9]. As a representative bulk-synchronous algorithm, we utilize an explicit time implementation of the 2D heat equation as a simple representative stencil computation. Following [5], we refer to the traditional bulk synchronous implementation as the *classic* algorithm. Each experiment is parameterized by the number of timesteps, nsteps, the number of processes, nprocs, and the computation time for a single timestep in seconds, C. While C is determined by other underlying algorithmic features, C is a more useful quantity since we are ultimately concerned with the runtimes of bulk-synchronous codes.

The experiments in this section are carried out on the Argonne Leadership Computing Facility's Cetus machine; an IBM BG/Q with 1600 MHz PowerPC A2 cores, 1 GB RAM per core, 16 cores per node, and a 5D Torus Proprietary Network interconnect. Each experiment uses a stencil size of $2,500^2$ points per process which resulted in the classic algorithm step duration of $C = 0.626$ s. Furthermore each experiment is run on $5,016$ processes, for nsteps $= 100$. All communication uses the eager protocol, and MPI asynchronous progress is enabled so as to avoid analyzing the complicating secondary impacts of asynchrony on rendezvous handshakes and other pieces of communication overhead.

3.1   Experiment 1: The Impact of Asynchrony

As a first step, we measure the impact of asynchrony on the runtime of the classic algorithm for two different detour durations, $T = 5C$ and $T = 10C$ using a value $\pi = T$. Figure 2 shows these results for the full range of asynchrony, from completely synchronous noise ($\alpha = 0.0$) to completely asynchronous noise ($\alpha = 1.0$).

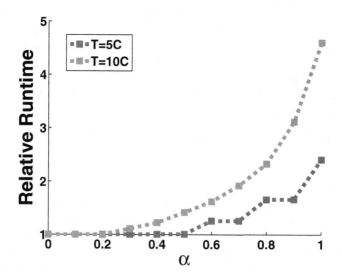

Fig. 2. The Relative Runtime of the classic algorithm for various levels of asynchrony, α. Relative Runtime is just the runtime of each data point divided by the runtime of the very first data point for each curve (where $\alpha = 0$, $T = 5C$ and $T = 10C$, respectively). In these experiments $\pi = T$, and experiments where $T = 5C$ and $10C$ are plotted.

The curves in Fig. 2 illustrate a few important characteristics of asynchrony. The most obvious is that as asynchrony approaches its maximum setting, performance degrades sharply. It provides a clear illustration of the massive impact which subtle mechanisms of computational noise can have on application performance.

In addition, the rate at which asynchrony, α, degrades the performance of the classic algorithm depends strongly on the detour duration, T. When $T = 5C$, asynchrony has almost an imperceivable impact on the performance of the classic algorithm when $\alpha \leq 0.5$. For $T = 10C$, the threshold of perceivable performance degradation occurs for $\alpha > 0.2$. The differences in these thresholds with respect to α masks their equivalence with respect to αT. When $\alpha = 0.2$ and $\alpha = 0.5$ for $T = 10C$ and $T = 5C$ respectively, $\alpha T = 2C$ in both cases. Moreover for both curves, any $\alpha T > 2C$ results in an increase in the runtime of the classic algorithm relative to its runtime in the presence of synchronous noise. It makes sense that αT is the point of similarity in the performance between the 2 curves given that the asynchrony of both is set by αT given by Eq. (1).

All of these observations point to the fact that for a given process of the classic algorithm, if the lag on an odd process is greater than its neighbor's by 2 steps worth of computation time, this detour will be 'felt' by processes beyond it. A difference of $2C$ between neighboring η represents a threshold beyond which the effects of detours propagate from the processes on which they occur to their neighboring processes. We therefore refer to the quantity, $2C$, as the 'propagation threshold' of the classic algorithm.

Finally, Fig. 2 points out the discrete nature in which asynchrony degrades performance. For the curve of runtimes where $T = 5C$, one can see that when $\alpha > 0.5$, the increase in runtime of the classic algorithm as asynchrony is increased proceeds in a stepwise manner. This can be explained as follows. When $T = 5C$, and α is increased above 0.5, the runtime of the classic algorithm only increases when $\frac{\alpha T}{C}$ yields an integer. Stated in other words, αT must equal an integer number of step durations of the classic algorithm in order for increases in asynchrony to have a noticeable impact on performance. The reason this characteristic is not seen for $T = 10C$, is because for every increase in α, where $\alpha = 0.2, 0.3, ..., 0.9, 1.0$, αT is equal to a monotonically increasing integer number of step durations of the classic algorithm.

These fascinating results, indicate that while noise on a given process may effect that process' performance, this effect will not propagate beyond itself unless the noise has very specific characteristics. In particular, the detour durations, T, of a given noise profile need to be greater than $2C$, and they need to be integer multiples of the step duration of the nearest neighbor bulk-synchronous algorithm in question. There are therefore significant degrees of freedom for these types of algorithms with respect to the manifestations of noise which they can tolerate.

3.2 Experiment 2: Using Frequency to Dampen the Impact of Asynchrony

In this experiment, we examine the effects that the frequency of detours has on the performance of the classic algorithm for both completely synchronous noise and completely asynchronous noise ($\alpha = 0.0$ and $\alpha = 1.0$ respectively). Here, frequency is simply the inverse period between detours ($\frac{1}{\pi}$). The results of these experiments are plotted in Fig. 3. The figure plots the period between detours,

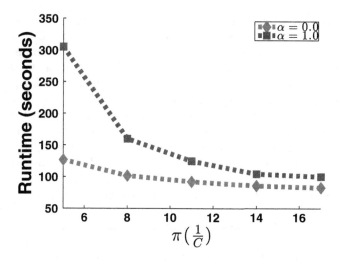

Fig. 3. The Runtime of the classic algorithm, given a range of constant period detours. π is plotted in units of $\frac{1}{C}$. Every simulation has the same detour duration throughout with a value of $T = 5C$.

π on the horizontal axis in units of $\frac{1}{C}$, and runtimes of the classic algorithm on the vertical axis.

The most obvious observation of Fig. 3 is that, when $\pi > T$, the impact of noise on application performance is significantly dampened. Recall that $T = 5C$, and therefore the leftmost data points in Fig. 3 plot points where $\pi = T$. As periods between detours, π, increases beyond the duration of detours themselves, the impact of each type of noise significantly decreases. The curve plotting the runtimes of completely asynchronous noise ($\alpha = 1.0$) provides the most striking illustration of this observation. The runtimes given by this curve approach those of the runtime of completely synchronous noise at the point when $\pi \approx 15C$.

Known statistics about present day state of the art machines tend to have fault rates whose periods are typically many times larger than their duration [10]. If these faults propagate linearly to the application layer, and if they provide any indication of what can be expected on future machines, asynchrony may be of small concern to HPC scientists of the future. However, how reliable these assumptions are, is still very much an open question.

3.3   Experiment 3: Using Asynchrony to Understand Gaussian Noise

In this experiment, we return to the original question – can we explain a bulk-synchronous algorithm's performance in the presence of Gaussian distributed noise? We replace the constant frequency detours employed in previous experiments with randomly sampled spacings. Furthermore, the lag on each process (formerly given by Eq. (1)) is given by sampling from a uniform distribution, seeded by the process rank. After the first detour, a Gaussian distribution is sampled at the end of each detour. Experiments with an appropriately chosen distribution mean, μ and standard deviation, σ, are performed and their runtimes are overlaid with those given by Fig. 3. This allows us to examine how much of the performance degradation experienced by the classic algorithm in the presence of random noise is captured by the mechanisms of asynchrony presented in Sect. 2. The results of these experiments are given in Fig. 4.

Figure 4a and b plot runtimes of the classic algorithm against the period, π, of constant frequency noise and the average period, μ, of Gaussian distributed noise. These periods are plotted in units of $\frac{1}{C}$. Every curve employs the same detour duration, $T = 5C$. Furthermore, each figure plots 2 constant frequency curves, and 1 Gaussian distributed frequency curve. The constant frequency curves display runtimes for completely synchronous and completely asynchronous noise ($\alpha = 0.0$ and $\alpha = 1.0$, respectively). The Gaussian distributed curve displays runtimes in the presence of Gaussian distributed noise with a standard deviation $\sigma = \frac{3C}{2} \approx \frac{T}{3}$.

The only difference between Fig. 4a and b, is that in Fig. 4a there is effectively no limit on the number of detours that can occur over the course of a simulation for every curve plotted. Figure 4b on the other hand limits the number of detours that can occur for the curve whose standard deviation, $\sigma = \frac{3C}{2}$. The limitation is set according to the number of detours incurred for the corresponding simulation of completely asynchronous constant frequency noise. In other words, if an execution of the classic algorithm in the presence of completely asynchronous noise ($\alpha = 1.0$) indicates that each process experienced X detours on average, when a similar experiment is performed for Gaussian noise (i.e. when the experiment where $\mu = \pi$ is performed), the number of detours allowed on

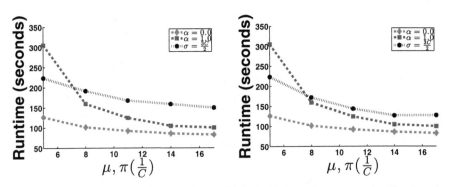

(a) Deterministic asynchrony compared to Gaussian noise without limits on the number of detours. (b) Deterministic asynchrony compared to Gaussian noise with limits on the number of detours.

Fig. 4. The Runtime of the classic algorithm, given a range of constant period detours and random period detours (with a constant period of π and an average period of μ respectively). μ and π are plotted on the same axis in units of $\frac{1}{C}$. This allows for a comparison between deterministic noise simulations with predefined levels of asynchrony and nondeterministic noise simulations with less predictable levels of asynchrony. Every simulation has the same detour duration throughout with a value of $T = 5C$.

each process is limited by X. The reason we do this is to remove the secondary effects on the frequency of detours which the standard deviation might have on Gaussian distributed noise simulations. Because these simulations are relatively small (nsteps = 100), we cannot necessarily assume that a law of large numbers applies. The goal of removing these secondary effects is to isolate the elements of asynchrony which impact the performance of the classic algorithm, and to test how well our model represents this mechanism.

What is immediately clear from Fig. 4 is that the model of asynchrony presented in Sect. 2 is limited in its explanatory power. The runtimes of the classic algorithm for the simulation of Gaussian noise are not bounded by the runtimes of simulations which experienced completely asynchronous noise ($\alpha = 1.0$). This is true for both the detour bounded and unbounded simulations. While it is clear that our model of asynchrony does not capture all of the complexities of the performance of the classic algorithm, we still believe that asynchrony is responsible for the gap between our expectations and the performance realities illustrated by Fig. 4; there is simply a more complex model of asynchrony underlying these results.

One way in which such a model might manifest itself is illustrated by Fig. 5. Figure 5 illustrates how the asynchrony caused by Gaussian noise may not be entirely captured by the model of asynchronous noise presented in Sect. 2. The vertical black lines in the figure indicate the progress of a simulation of constant frequency detours with an asynchrony, $\alpha = 1.0$, and $\pi > T$. The red lines indicate

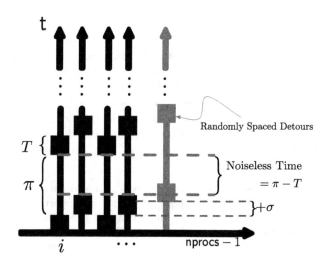

Fig. 5. An illustration of additional manifestations of asynchrony that could explain the runtimes of the classic algorithm in the presence of Gaussian noise. The vertical black lines indicate the progress of a simulation of constant frequency detours with an asynchrony, $\alpha = 1.0$, and $\pi > T$. The red line indicates randomly distributed detours. As can be seen the time in which every process usually proceeds in a completely noiseless fashion, is offset by a randomly placed detour (Colour figure online).

randomly distributed detours. The illustration of Fig. 5 further shows that what is completely noiseless execution time for constant frequency asynchronous noise is diminished by the randomly occurring detour in the $\pi - T$ time window. This explanation further explains why completely asynchronous noise *does* bound the performance of the classic algorithm for the case where $\pi = \mu = T$. In this case, the time window of $\pi - T = 0$. Understanding this data, and our hypothesis requires further analysis and research.

4   Conclusions

This study has presented a model for asynchronous noise, and examined the impact that such noise has on the runtimes of nearest neighbor synchronizing bulk-synchronous codes. The analysis of these runtimes has indicated that asynchrony acts as a bounding property of the performance of bulk-synchronous algorithms in the presence of arbitrary noise profiles, be they deterministic or non-deterministic. That having been said, the model of asynchrony developed in this study cannot explain all of the performance observed. The model's limitations need to be further explored, and refined. The power of these results, and the promise of further research in this vein is that we have identified a deterministic mechanism of what more often than not results from very randomly occurring sources of performance degradation in HPC applications. Understanding this mechanism gives some insight into how best to work around it.

Liscense

Acknowledgements. This research used resources of the Argonne Leadership Computing Facility at Argonne National Laboratory, which is supported by the Office of Science of the U.S. Department of Energy under contract DE-AC02-06CH11357.

This research used the University of Delaware's *Chimera* computer, funded by U.S. National Science Foundation award CNS-0958512. S.F. Siegel was supported by NSF award CCF-0953210.

References

1. Agarwal, S., Garg, R., Vishnoi, N.K.: The impact of noise on the scaling of collectives: a theoretical approach. In: Bader, D.A., Parashar, M., Sridhar, V., Prasanna, V.K. (eds.) HiPC 2005. LNCS, vol. 3769, pp. 280–289. Springer, Heidelberg (2005)

2. Beckman, P., Iskra, K., Yoshii, K., Coghlan, S.: The influence of operating systems on the performance of collective operations at extreme scale. In: 2006 IEEE International Conference on Cluster Computing, pp. 1–12 (2006)

3. Brown, D.L., Messina, P., Beckman, P., Keyes, D., Vetter, J., Anitescu, M., Bell, J., Brightwell, R., Chamberlain, B., Estep, D., Geist, A., Hendrickson, B., Heroux, M., Lusk, R., Morrison, J., Pinar, A., Shalf, J., Shephard, M.: Cross cutting technologies for computing at the exascale. Technical report, U.S. Department of Energy (DOE) Office of Advanced Scientific Computing Research and the National Nuclear Security Administration, June 2010

4. Garg, R., De, P.: Impact of Noise on scaling of collectives: an empirical evaluation. In: Robert, Y., Parashar, M., Badrinath, R., Prasanna, V.K. (eds.) HiPC 2006. LNCS, vol. 4297, pp. 460–471. Springer, Heidelberg (2006)

5. Hammouda, A., Siegel, A., Siegel, S.: Noise-tolerant explicit stencil computations for nonuniform process execution rates. ACM Trans. Parallel Comput. (2014, Accepted)

6. Hoefler, T., Schneider, T., Lumsdaine, A.: Characterizing the influence of system noise on large-scale applications by simulation. In: Proceedings of the 2010 ACM/IEEE International Conference for High Performance Computing, Networking, Storage and Analysis, SC 2010, pp. 1–11. IEEE Computer Society, Washington, DC, USA (2010). http://dx.doi.org/10.1109/SC.2010.12

7. Lipman, J., Stout, Q.F.: Analysis of delays caused by local synchronization. SIAM J. Comput. **39**(8), 3860–3884 (2010). http://dx.doi.org/10.1137/080723090

8. Petrini, F., Kerbyson, D.J., Pakin, S.: The case of the missing supercomputer performance: Achieving optimal performance on the 8,192 processors of ASCI Q. In: Proceedings of the 2003 ACM/IEEE conference on Supercomputing, SC 2003, pp. 55. ACM, New York, NY, USA (2003). http://doi.acm.org/10.1145/1048935.1050204

9. Siegel, A., Siegel, S., Hammouda, A.: Sythetic noise utilities (2014). https://bitbucket.org/adamhammouda3/iutils

10. Snir, M., Wisniewski, R.W., Abraham, J.A., Adve, S.V., Bagchi, S., Balaji, P., Belak, J., Bose, P., Cappello, F., Carlson, B., Chien, A.A., Coteus, P., Debardeleben, N.A., Diniz, P., Engelmann, C., Erez, M., Fazzari, S., Geist, A., Gupta, R., Johnson, F., Krishnamoorthy, S., Leyffer, S., Liberty, D., Mitra, S., Munson, T.S., Schreiber, R., Stearley, J., Hensbergen, E.V.: Addressing failures in exascale computing*. Int. J. High Perform. Comput. (2013)

11. Tsafrir, D., Etsion, Y., Feitelson, D.G., Kirkpatrick, S.: System noise, OS clock ticks, and fine-grained parallel applications. In: Proceedings of the 19th annual international conference on Supercomputing, ICS 2005, pp. 303–312. ACM, New York, NY, USA (2005). http://doi.acm.org/10.1145/1088149.1088190

12. Vishnoi, N.K.: The impact of noise on the scaling of collectives: the nearest neighbor model [extended abstract]. In: Aluru, S., Parashar, M., Badrinath, R., Prasanna, V.K. (eds.) HiPC 2007. LNCS, vol. 4873, pp. 476–487. Springer, Heidelberg (2007)

Memory Usage Optimizations for Online Event Analysis

Tobias Hilbrich[1], Joachim Protze[2,3], Michael Wagner[1], Matthias S. Müller[2,3], Martin Schulz[4(✉)], Bronis R. de Supinski[4], and Wolfgang E. Nagel[1]

[1] Technische Universität Dresden, 01062 Dresden, Germany
{tobias.hilbrich,michael.wagner2,wolfgang.nagel}@tu-dresden.de
[2] RWTH Aachen University, 52056 Aachen, Germany
{protze,mueller}@rz.rwth-aachen.de
[3] JARA – High-Performance Computing, 52062 Aachen, Germany
[4] Lawrence Livermore National Laboratory, Livermore, CA 94551, USA
{schulzm,bronis}@llnl.gov

Abstract. Tools are essential for application developers and system support personnel during tasks such as performance optimization and debugging of massively parallel applications. An important class are event-based tools that analyze relevant events during the runtime of an application, e.g., function invocations or communication operations. We develop a parallel tools infrastructure that supports both the observation and analysis of application events at runtime. Some analyses—e.g., deadlock detection algorithms—require complex processing and apply to many types of frequently occurring events. For situations where the rate at which an application generates new events exceeds the processing rate of the analysis, we experience tool instability or even failures, e.g., memory exhaustion. Tool infrastructures must provide means to avoid or mitigate such situations. This paper explores two such techniques: first, a heuristic that selects events to receive and process next; second, a *pause* mechanism that temporarily suspends the execution of an application. An application study with applications from the SPEC MPI2007 benchmark suite and the NAS parallel benchmarks evaluates these techniques at up to 16,384 processes and illustrates how they avoid memory exhaustion problems that limited the applicability of a runtime correctness tool in the past.

1 Introduction

High Performance Computing (HPC) architectures feature increasing compute core counts, such as the Sequoia system at the Lawrence Livermore National Laboratory with more than 1.5 million cores. This trend challenges both developers of HPC applications as well as the maintainers of tools that aid these developers. Especially tools that operate at application runtime must provide sufficient scalability to be applicable for application runs with large core counts.

The rights of this work are transferred to the extent transferable according to title 17 §105 U.S.C.

ⓒ Springer International Publishing Switzerland 2015 (outside the US)
S. Markidis and E. Laure (Eds.): EASC 2014, LNCS 8759, pp. 110–121, 2015.
DOI: 10.1007/978-3-319-15976-8_8

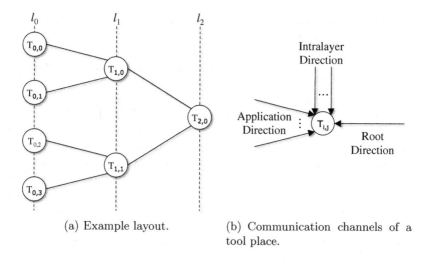

(a) Example layout.

(b) Communication channels of a tool place.

Fig. 1. Illustration of a runtime tool with a TBON layout.

We develop the Generic Tools Infrastructure (GTI) [8] to simplify the development of such scalable runtime tools, in particular tools that analyze large numbers of events (function invocations or communication events) in Message Passing Interface (MPI) [15] applications. Those tools analyze events for use cases such as performance optimization or debugging. Performance analysis tools like Vampir [17] and Scalasca [5] use traces to store events during the runtime of an application and then apply a post-mortem analysis. However, tool exclusive computing resources and a Tree-Based Overlay Network (TBON) abstraction allow tools built upon GTI to analyze such event data already during the runtime of an application; in other words online.

GTI uses extra processes as additional compute resources for the tool itself. These tool processes—called *places* in GTI—can analyze events outside of the critical path of the application. Additionally, GTI organizes places in hierarchy layers that can apply stepwise event analysis (TBON layout), e.g., all application processes provide an event with an integer value and the hierarchy layers sum these events up until the root of the layout retrieves a global sum. This combination of event offloading, analysis outside the critical path, and hierarchic event analysis enables wide ranges of scalable tools. Figure 1(a) illustrates the layout of a GTI tool for four application processes—represented as circles with labels $T_{0,0}$–$T_{0,3}$—and three tool places $T_{1,0}$, $T_{1,1}$, and $T_{2,0}$. The lines between the circles indicate the communication channels for events, e.g., the application process $T_{0,0}$ would usually forward events to tool place $T_{1,0}$ for analysis. The tool places can analyze events from the application processes, but also use the communication capabilities of the layout to exchange information with each other.

The GTI-based tool MUST [7] analyzes all communication operations of an application to reveal MPI usage errors. The tool applies a comparatively expensive event analysis as part of its deadlock detection scheme. Thus, the envent handling and analysis cost of MUST may exceed the original cost of the communication operations on the application. Under such a scenario an online event analysis tool like MUST can consume increasing amounts of memory and may fail due to memory exhaustion. Even on a compute system with 24 GB of main memory per compute node—shared between 12 cores—MUST repeatedly exhausted memory for one benchmark application in a study of its deadlock detection capabilities [7]. This paper describes and studies two techniques for TBON-based event analysis tools to avoid memory exhaustion problems. Specifically, these techniques avoid storing data into files since the use of the I/O subsystem imposes further challenges at scale [11, 22]. This research may particularly enable new tool workflows for Exascale-level compute systems that increase challenges around massively parallel I/O system use. An increasing use of online tools could circumvent the challenges that these systems impose onto traditional post-mortem tools.

Section 2 first presents related work and Sect. 3 then details our assumptions for the communication channels of a TBON and refines our problem statement. Section 4 contains our first technique, a heuristic that provides tool places a communication channel selection that offers a tune-able selection between performance and memory consumption. Section 5 then describes our second technique that temporarily pauses the execution of an application to let a tool "catch up" with its event analysis. We implement these techniques in our tool infrastructure GTI and evaluate it with the runtime MPI correctness tool MUST that previously failed for some SPEC MPI2007 benchmarks. An application study with MPI2007 and the NAS Parallel Benchmarks (NPB) evaluates our techniques at up to 16,384 processes and avoids memory exhaustion in practice (Sect. 6).

2   Related Work

We describe techniques that overcome deficiencies [7] in the GTI-based tool MUST. These deficiencies result from online event analysis on large event counts where the analysis requires increasing amounts of memory for some series of events. The techniques that we describe apply to tools that handle events in TBONs. Besides MUST, various existing tools and tool infrastructures for high performance computing use TBONs, but often operate on very few events per MPI process. Examples for performance optimization include Periscope [6] that applies an analysis on profiling data for application phases; and TAUoverMR-Net [18] that analyses profiling data at user specified execution points or for periodic time intervals. Debugging tools like STAT [1] retrieve call stack information from all processes to represent a global execution state, this data could hardly exhaust memory on any node of the TBON layout. Implementations of our techniques are not bound to GTI, but can also be used to improve the reliability of infrastructures such as MRNet [20], CBTF [13], STCI [4] or SCI [12].

MALP [3] also targets the analysis of large event counts at scale. However, its analyses provide profiling-based performance reports for which a constant amount of memory suffices to handle any event series. Event sizes that increase with application scale [14] are a related problem that can limit the applicability of an online tool.

File system traces represent an alternative to our techniques that target reduced memory needs during event analysis. Our analyses could store temporary event information into traces to avoid memory exhaustion. Tools such as Vampir [17] and Scalasca [5] successfully employ traces for their performance analysis. However, file systems can impose scalability challenges [11,22] as well. Various approaches exist to mitigate the effect of this bottleneck, e.g., trace reduction [21], trace compression [19], and I/O forwarding [11].

3   Channels and Memory

Figure 1(a) illustrates a TBON layout. For GTI, application processes and tool places use up to three different communication directions as Fig. 1(b) illustrates. The *application* direction allows a place to receive events that travel from the application processes towards the root, the *root* direction allows a place to receive events that travel from the root towards the application processes (usually control and steering), and the *intralayer* direction provides GTI tools a point-to-point communication means within a hierarchy layer. The latter communication direction facilitates tool analyses such as point-to-point message matching for which pure TBON layouts could limit scalability [10]. The arrows in Fig. 1(b) illustrate that tool places can probe any communication channel from any of these three communication directions to receive a new event. Each communication channel is bidirectional and has a certain event capacity. That is, if an application process or a tool place sends an event over a channel it can continue its execution before the receiver side handled the event, as long as the capacity of the channel suffices to store the new event. If a communication channel reaches its capacity it will block any subsequent send operations until the receiver side drains some events from the channel. In GTI, this capacity depends on the selection of the communication system, which can either be optimized for bandwidth, offering high capacities, or latency, offering only low capacities.

Analysis algorithms such as point-to-point message matching [10] or deadlock analysis [7], as well as tool infrastructure services such as order preserving event aggregation [9] can consume increasing amounts of memory if newly received events do not satisfy certain conditions. In such scenarios, the channel selection of a tool place can heavily impact the memory consumption of a tool. We illustrate this with MPI point-to-point message matching as an example analysis that searches for pairs of send and receive events with matching message envelopes. If a new send/receive event arrives and no matching receive/send is available, then the analysis stores information on the new event in a matching table, i.e., memory consumption increases. Otherwise, if a new send/receive event completes a pair—a matching receive/send event was present in the matching table—the analysis can remove the latter event from the table. Thus, the memory consumption of the analysis decreases. This analysis enables correctness tools like MUST to implement MPI type matching checks that can reveal incorrect data transfers.

```
MPI_Comm_size(&p)
MPI_Comm_rank(&r)
assert (p%3 == 0)
for i ∈ {1, 2, ..., iterations} do
    switch r%3 do
        case 0
            MPI_Send(to:(r + 1))
        end
        case 1
            MPI_Recv(from:(r − 1))
            MPI_Recv(from:(r + 1))
        end
        case 2
            MPI_Send(to:(r − 1))
        end
    end
end
```

```
MPI_Comm_size(&p)
MPI_Comm_rank(&r)
for i ∈ {1, 2, ..., iterations} do
    MPI_Isend(to:(r + 1)%p, &req)
    MPI_Recv(from:(r − 1)%p)
    MPI_Wait(&req)
end
```

(a) Homogeneous.

(b) Process behavior differs.

Fig. 2. Communication pattern examples (pseudo code).

As an example, a single tool place could receive events from all application processes in order to match MPI point-to-point operations; in other words, the tool uses a TBON that consists of the application processes and a root. In that case, the single tool place exclusively uses the application communication direction and only needs to select which application process to receive an event from. A round-robin scheme efficiently handles homogeneous applications where all MPI processes execute similar events, such as the example pattern in Fig. 2(a). Given that all channels provide an event when probed, the matching table of the point-to-point matching analysis would store at most p operations for a round-robin channel selection. The analysis reaches this peak after it handled an MPI_Isend event from each process. At the same time, application processes can exhibit different MPI operations such as in the communication pattern of Fig. 2(b). This example[1] uses process triples where two processes send to the third process, which in turn receives the two send operations. A round-robin scheme would behave poorly for this example since one process in each triple issues twice as many operations than the other processes. The matching table could use up to $iterations \cdot (\frac{p}{3})$ entries for unmatched send operations for the round-robin approach. In practices, functional decomposition and border processes for domain decompositions can cause different MPI operation workloads, such a in the example of Fig. 2(b).

In summary, the memory consumption of an analysis depends on the channel selection scheme of the tool places, the communication pattern of the application, the capacity of the communication channels, and the analysis algorithm.

---

[1] Uses numbers of processes that are a multiple of three.

The previous example illustrated the impact of the communication pattern. The capacity of a communication channel together with the number of synchronization points in the application also impacts the memory consumption of tool analyses. Once a channel reaches its capacity, no further events can be processed causing the application process to be blocked. This will then indirectly block other processes in their synchronization operations, leading to a cascading effect. Blocked processes can continue their execution once higher hierarchy layers of the tool drain some events from the communication channels.

4   Selection Heuristic

To avoid this kind of impact on application execution, we develop and implement two techniques in GTI. The first one is a heuristic solution to select a communication channel when a place tries to receive a new event. The heuristic targets low-overhead channel selection with a consideration of memory usage. On each tool place, a penalty score for each communication channel represents how often events from this channel increased memory consumption as well as how often the channel failed to provide an event when probed. The score starts at 0 and GTI adds a penalty of α when an event increases memory consumption and a penalty of β when a channel failed to provide an event. Places sort all channels with increasing penalty into a list. When a place probes for a new event it starts with the first channel in the list. Channels that fail to provide an event receive the penalty increase of β and the place advances to the next channel in the list. If a channel provides an event, the place processes the event and any analysis can return feedback whether the event increased their memory consumption via an API. If so, the place applies the penalty of α to the channel that provided the event, otherwise the score remains unchanged. Afterwards, a place reorders the list and probes the first channel in the list again.

This heuristic targets a flexible selection between low memory consumption and low overhead where the values of β and α allow an adaption between the two goals. A selection of $\alpha > 0$ and $\beta = 0$ would only organize channels based on their memory impact and a selection of $\alpha = 0$ and $\beta > 0$ would prefer channels that *usually* provide events as to avoid unsuccessful probes. Additionally, the number of channels along the application direction is usually low and about constant across scales (most TBON-based tools use constant fan-ins across scale), while the number of channels along the intralayer communication direction usually increases with scale. The organization of increasing numbers of channels in a priority list would impact the performance of the selection heuristic at scale. Thus, GTI uses a wildcard receive semantic for the intralayer channel and represents it as a single entry in its channel lists.

5   Application Pause

The channel selection heuristic attempts to receive events that will not increase memory, but bases its selection on past behavior. GTI incorporates a second technique to avoid memory exhaustion when the heuristic fails to restrict memory usage. GTI-based tools can request an application pause such that application processes will not generate new events. A place should invoke such a request if its memory usage exceeds a threshold σ. Once the application is paused, tool places can process all existing events to reduce their memory usage. For applications that synchronize within some regular interval, any intermediate execution state of the application should have a limited number of open operations (e.g., unmatched communications) for which analyses need to store information. As a result, memory consumption of analyses can decrease towards the memory demand for these open operations, which should be far below the original threshold that caused a place to request an application pause. Once the memory usage of a place that requested an application pause decreases below a second threshold σ' ($\sigma' < \sigma$), it will request that the application should be resumed.

GTI handles this technique with events that any place can inject. These tool specific events travel either along the application or the root communication direction. Four events implement the technique:

– `requestPause`:
  • A tool place injects this event if an analysis exceeds its memory threshold,
  • Tool places forward these events towards the root of the TBON,
– `broadcastPause`:
  • The root of the TBON injects this event when it received one more `requestPause` events than `requestResume` events,
  • The root broadcasts the event towards the application processes,
  • When an application process receives this event it waits until it receives a *broadcastResume* event.
– `requestResume`:
  • Tool places inject this event if they injected a `requestPause` event and their memory usage decreases below σ'
  • Tool places forward these events towards the root of the TBON,
– `broadcastResume`:
  • The root of the TBON injects this event when it received as many `request Resume` events as it received `requestPause` events,
  • The root broadcasts the event towards the application processes.

This handling continuously votes for an application pause. The root of the TBON manages the voting and holds an application pause until all places that previously requested a pause agree to resuming the application. The implementation in GTI uses a scalable event aggregation on all levels of the TBON to combine `requestPause` and `requestResume` events.

6   Application Study

We use the Juqueen system at the Forschungszentrum Jülich and the NAS Parallel Benchmarks (NPB) [2] (v3.3-MPI) for our measurements. This Blue Gene/Q system features 28,672 nodes with 16 cores and 16 GB of main memory each.

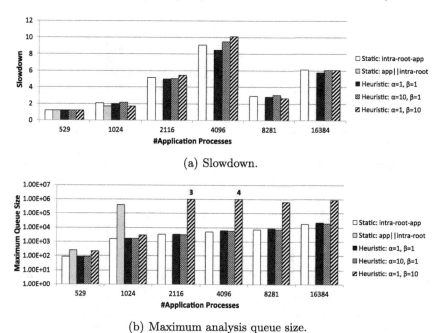

(a) Slowdown.

(b) Maximum analysis queue size.

Fig. 3. Channel selection strategy comparison for NPB *sp* on Juqueen.

We implement our techniques in GTI and use the distributed deadlock detection in MUST as an expensive tool analysis that keeps a queue of active MPI operations for deadlock detection. We use the size of this queue to both apply the α penalty of our heuristic and to request an application pause, where we use values of $\sigma = 10^6$ events and $\sigma' = \frac{\sigma}{2}$ events in all runs with our techniques. As kernel we select *sp* since it combines high communication frequency with longer runtime. We use problem size D at up to 4,096 processes and size E at up to 16,384 processes; hence, the dip at 8,192 in Fig. 3(a). Figure 3 shows the application slowdown (as runtime with MUST divided by the runtime of a reference run) and the maximum queue size of MUST's analysis for increasing scales. We compare five different channel selections where we use two static approaches (previous version of GTI) and three selections with our new techniques that differ in their choices for α and β. The static selection *intra-root-app* selects channels in rounds where it first tries to receive an event from the intralayer direction, afterwards—irrespective of whether it received an event—it tries to receive from the root direction, and finally it tries to receive from the application direction. This scheme is a compromise between a performance impact due to unnecessary probes and serving all three directions. The second static selection *app||intra-root* receives events from the application direction whenever possible and only investigates the other directions if no application event is available. This scheme tries to avoid blocked application processes that satisfy their communication channel capacity towards low tool overhead. The selections with our techniques

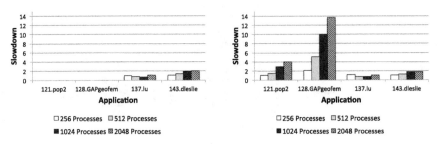

(a) Slowdown for static selection with *intra-root-app*.

(b) Slowdown for our approach with $\alpha = 1$, $\beta = 1$, $\sigma = 10^6$, and $\sigma' = \frac{\sigma}{2}$.

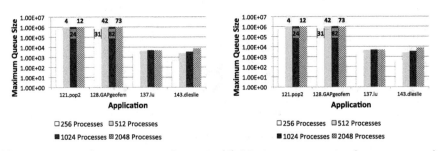

(c) Maximum analysis queue size for static selection with *inta-root-app*.

(d) Maximum queue size for our approach with $\alpha = 1$, $\beta = 1$, $\sigma = 10^6$, and $\sigma' = \frac{\sigma}{2}$.

Fig. 4. Channel selection strategy comparison for MPI2007 on Sierra.

use $\alpha = \beta = 1$ as a compromise between performance and memory usage, $\alpha = 10$ with $\beta = 1$ to prefer lower memory use, and $\alpha = 1$ with $\beta = 10$ to prefer channels that usually provide events towards low tool overhead.

The static selection *app*‖*intra-root* already uses exhaustive amounts of memory at 2,116 processes and causes an out-of-memory crash for this scale. This selection fails to probe communication channels that offer events that would decrease memory usage in practice. A selection with *intra-root-app* provides low queue sizes for the homogeneous communication pattern of *sp*, but issues many irrelevant probes on communication channels. Thus, it causes higher overheads than the heuristic selection with $\alpha = \beta = 1$, especially at 4,096 and 16,384 processes. The latter heuristic selection provides the best results for *sp* overall. It causes marginally higher queue lengths than *intra-root-app* or $\alpha = 1$ with $\beta = 10$, but has the lowest overall slowdown. A selection of $\alpha = 10$ with $\beta = 1$ can provide good performance, e.g., at 1,024 processes, but quickly causes excessive queue lengths that trigger the application pause technique at 2,116 and 4,096 application processes with 3 and 4 pauses respectively. The application pauses along with the increased memory usage increase tool overheads for scales above 1,024 processes.

A second set of experiments uses the Sierra system at the Lawrence Livermore National Laboratory, a Linux cluster with 1,944 nodes of two 6 core Xeon 5660 processors each (24 GB of main memory per node, and a QDR InfiniBand interconnect). We run the *lref* data set of the SPEC MPI2007 [16] (v2.0) benchmark suite on up to 2,048 cores[2] on this system to study less homogeneous applications. Particularly, these applications are derived from real world applications and provide a challenging test case. We select the applications *121.pop2*, *128.GAPgeofem*, *137.lu*, and *143.dleslie* for our runs since they particularly stress MUST or even caused memory exhaustion previously. Figure 4(a) and (c) present application slowdown and maximum queue length for our previous version of GTI and MUST that uses the static selection *intra-root-app*. The irregular communications in both *121.pop2* and *128.GAPgeofem* cause MUST to exhaust memory even at 256 processes. Figure 4(b) and (d) present application slowdowns and maximum queue sizes for our techniques with $\alpha = \beta = 1$. The heuristic suffices to handle *121.pop2* at 256 processes without the application pause technique, i.e., it adapts better than *intra-root-app* to the communication pattern of this application. The application pause technique avoids memory exhaustion for the remaining runs of *121.pop2* and *128.GAPgeofem*. The numbers above/below the bars in Fig. 4(d) indicate the number of pauses that each run uses. The figure also highlights that processing all remaining non-application events during an application pause does not cause excessive increases in the maximum queue size for the MPI2007 applications. The highest queue size for these runs was about 5 % above σ.

7   Conclusions

We present two techniques to avoid memory exhaustion in online analysis tools for high performance computing. These techniques facilitate use cases where complex tool analysis algorithms are used to process a large numbers of events. Our first technique provides a heuristic that selects a communication channel by using feedback from the tool infrastructure as well as the analysis itself to rank channels in a priority list. A performance study with up to 16,384 application processes shows that this heuristic provides an event selection that causes no memory exhaustion for homogeneous applications and that it reduces tool overhead compared to static selection approaches. Notably, this technique allows the tool to analyze applications such as *121.pop2* at 256 processes where the static selection already exhausts memory.

Our second technique uses the management capabilities of a TBON to pause the execution of all application processes if a tool analysis uses large amounts of memory. Once the application pauses its execution a tool can analyze all events in the system in order to reduce the memory consumption of the analyses. This mechanism handles cases where the heuristic channel selection would

---

[2] The *lref* data set operates with up to 2,048 processes (http://www.spec.org/mpi/docs/faq.html#DataSetL).

exhaust memory otherwise and application studies on two different compute systems show its practicability. Particularly, this technique allows MUST to handle applications for which it previously failed, e.g., *121.pop2* and *128.GAPgeofem*. Thus, our approach increases the applicability of runtime correctness tools such as MUST.

We implement both techniques in the open source tool infrastructure GTI that targets efficient development of online tools. Increased scalability and availability of online tools for tasks such as performance analysis and debugging are an essential step to provide an alternative for trace-based tool workflows, which are increasingly impacted by I/O limitations.

Acknowledgments. We thank the ASC Tri-Labs and the Los Alamos National Laboratory for their friendly support. Part of this work was performed under the auspices of the U.S. Department of Energy by Lawrence Livermore National Laboratory under Contract DE-AC52-07NA27344. (LLNL-CONF-652119). This work has been supported by the CRESTA project that has received funding from the European Community's Seventh Framework Programme (ICT-2011.9.13) under Grant Agreement no. 287703.

References

1. Arnold, D.C., Ahn, D.H., de Supinski, B.R., Lee, G.L., Miller, B.P., Schulz, M.: Stack trace analysis for large scale debugging. In: International Parallel and Distributed Processing Symposium (2007)
2. Bailey, D.H., Dagum, L., Barszcz, E., Simon, H.D.: NAS parallel benchmark results. Technical report, IEEE Parallel and Distributed Technology (1992)
3. Besnard, J.-B., Pérache, M., Jalby, W.: Event streaming for online performance measurements reduction. In: 42nd International Conference on Parallel Processing, ICPP 2013, pp. 985–994 (2013)
4. Buntinas, D., Bosilca, G., Graham, R.L., Vallée, G., Watson, G.R.: A scalable tools communications infrastructure. In: Proceedings of the 2008 22nd International Symposium on High Performance Computing Systems and Applications, HPCS 2008, pp. 33–39. IEEE Computer Society, Washington (2008)
5. Geimer, M., Wolf, F., Wylie, B.J.N., Ábrahám, E., Becker, D., Mohr, B.: The Scalasca performance toolset architecture. Concurrency Comput. Pract. Exp. **22**(6), 702–719 (2010)
6. Gerndt, M., Fürlinger, K., Kereku, E.: Periscope: advanced techniques for performance analysis. In: Parallel Computing: Current and Future Issues of High-End Computing, Proceedings of the International Conference ParCo 2005, John von Neumann Institute for Computing Series, vol. 33. Central Institute for Applied Mathematics, Jülich (2005)
7. Hilbrich, T., de Supinski, B.R., Nagel, W.E., Protze, J., Baier, C., Müller, M.S.: Distributed wait state tracking for runtime MPI deadlock detection. In: Proceedings of SC13: International Conference for High Performance Computing, Networking, Storage and Analysis, SC 2013, pp. 16:1–16:12. ACM, New York (2013)
8. Hilbrich, T., Müller, M.S., de Supinski, B.R., Schulz, M., Nagel, W.E.: GTI: a generic tools infrastructure for event-based tools in parallel systems. In: Proceedings of the 2012 IEEE 26th International Parallel and Distributed Processing Symposium, IPDPS 2012, pp. 1364–1375. IEEE Computer Society, Washington (2012)

9. Hilbrich, T., Müller, M.S., Schulz, M., de Supinski, B.R.: Order preserving event aggregation in TBONs. In: Cotronis, Y., Danalis, A., Nikolopoulos, D.S., Dongarra, J. (eds.) EuroMPI 2011. LNCS, vol. 6960, pp. 19–28. Springer, Heidelberg (2011)

10. Hilbrich, T., Protze, J., de Supinski, B.R., Schulz, M., Müller, M.S., Nagel, W.E.: Intralayer communication for tree-based overlay networks. In: 42nd International Conference on Parallel Processing (ICPP), Fourth International Workshop on Parallel Software Tools and Tool Infrastructures, pp. 995–1003. IEEE Computer Society Press, Los Alamitos (2013)

11. Ilsche, T., Schuchart, J., Cope, J., Kimpe, D., Jones, T., Knüpfer, A., Iskra, K., Ross, R., Nagel, W.E., Poole, S.: Enabling event tracing at leadership-class scale through I/O forwarding middleware. In: Proceedings of the 21st International Symposium on High-Performance Parallel and Distributed Computing, HPDC 2012, pp. 49–60. ACM, New York (2012)

12. Jun, T.H., Watson, G.R.: Scalable Communication Infrastructure (2013). http://wiki.eclipse.org/PTP/designs/SCI Accessed 30 April 2013

13. Krell Institute. The Component Based Tool Infrastructure (2014). http://sourceforge.net/projects/cbtf/ Accessed 19 January 2014

14. Lee, G.L., Ahn, D.H., Arnold, D.C., de Supinski, B.R., Legendre, M., Miller, B.P., Schulz, M., Liblit, B.: Lessons learned at 208K: towards debugging millions of cores. In: Proceedings of the 2008 ACM/IEEE Conference on Supercomputing, SC 2008, pp. 26:1–26:9. IEEE Press, Piscataway (2008)

15. Message Passing Interface Forum. MPI: A Message-Passing Interface Standard, Version 3.0 (2012). http://www.mpi-forum.org/docs/mpi-3.0/mpi30-report.pdf Accessed 27 November 2013

16. Müller, M.S., van Waveren, M., Lieberman, R., Whitney, B., Saito, H., Kumaran, K., Baron, J., Brantley, W.C., Parrott, C., Elken, T., Feng, H., Ponder, C.: SPEC MPI2007 - an application benchmark suite for parallel systems using MPI. Concurrency Comput. Pract. Exp. **22**(2), 191–205 (2010)

17. Nagel, W.E., Arnold, A., Weber, M., Hoppe, H.C., Solchenbach, K.: VAMPIR: visualization and analysis of MPI resources. Supercomputer **12**(1), 69–80 (1996)

18. Nataraj, A., Malony, A.D., Morris, A., Arnold, D.C., Miller, B.P.: A framework for scalable, parallel performance monitoring. Concurrency Comput. Pract. Exp. **22**(6), 720–735 (2010)

19. Noeth, M., Mueller, F., Schulz, M., de Supinski, B.R.: Scalable compression and replay of communication traces in massively parallel environments. In: IEEE International Parallel and Distributed Processing Symposium, IPDPS 2007, pp. 69–70 (2007)

20. Roth, P.C., Arnold, D.C., Miller, B.P.: MRNet: a software-based multicast/reduction network for scalable tools. In: Proceedings of the 2003 ACM/IEEE Conference on Supercomputing, SC 2003. ACM, New York (2003)

21. Wagner, M., Knüpfer, A., Nagel, W.E.: Hierarchical memory buffering techniques for an in-memory event tracing extension to the open trace format 2. In: 42nd International Conference on Parallel Processing, ICPP 2013, pp. 970–976 (2013)

22. Wylie, B.J.N., Geimer, M., Mohr, B., Böhme, D., Szebenyi, Z., Wolf, F.: Large-scale performance analysis of Sweep3D with the Scalasca toolset. Parallel Process. Lett. **20**(04), 397–414 (2010)

Towards Detailed Exascale Application Analysis — Selective Monitoring and Visualisation

Jens Doleschal[✉], Thomas William, Bert Wesarg, Johannes Ziegenbalg, Holger Brunst, Andreas Knüpfer, and Wolfgang E. Nagel

ZIH, Technische Universität Dresden, 01062 Dresden, Germany
{jens.doleschal,thomas.william,bert.wesarg,johannes.ziegenbalg, holger.brunst,andreas.knuepfer,wolfgang.nagel}@zih.tu-dresden.de

Abstract. We introduce novel ideas involving aspect-oriented instrumentation, Multi-Faceted Program Monitoring, as well as novel techniques for a selective and detailed event-based application performance analysis, with an eye toward exascale. We give special attention to the spatial, temporal, and level-of-detail aspects of the three important phases of compile-time filtering, application execution, and runtime filtering. We use an event-based monitoring approach to allow selected and focused performance analysis.

Keywords: Multi-Faceted program monitoring · Aspect-oriented instrumentation · Selective event tracing · Vampir · Performance analysis

1 Introduction and Motivation

Today's leading edge HPC systems are composed of millions of homogeneous or even heterogeneous processing elements. Running applications efficiently in such highly parallel and complex systems requires orchestrating different levels of concurrency. Therefore, it will be necessary to discover performance bottlenecks originating from the increase of complexity of each level of concurrency and to correct them in the application source codes.

The state and the behaviour of an application over runtime can be observed by using instrumentation, by using a sampling approach or by a combination of both. The selection of the right technique for a given performance issue is always a trade-off between intrusion and the level of detail with emphasis on reducing the intrusiveness while providing enough information needed to detect different kinds of performance bottlenecks.

While sampling relies on its sampling frequency to gain information about the application, event-based monitoring only records information if a specific predefined event occurs, e.g., function entry/exit. The level of detail therefore depends on the events that should be monitored, their occurrence, and also their duration. Using event-based monitoring can result in detailed information, but as the level of detail increases, the intrusion will become more and more critical, especially when tiny and often-used functions are monitored, e.g., inline functions.

© Springer International Publishing Switzerland 2015
S. Markidis and E. Laure (Eds.): EASC 2014, LNCS 8759, pp. 122–129, 2015.
DOI: 10.1007/978-3-319-15976-8_9

Event-based and sampling information can be aggregated to statistical data of the application during runtime with various profiling approaches or recorded individually with tracing techniques. Profiling with its nature of summarization offers an opportunity to be extremely scalable, since the reduction of information can be done during the application runtime. Nevertheless, profiles may lack crucial information, e.g., about message runtimes and bandwidth, since message matching is usually infeasible during profiling. In contrast, event tracing records each event of a parallel application in detail. Thus, it allows capturing the dynamic interaction between thousands of concurrent processing elements, and it is possible to identify outliers from the regular behaviour. As a result, for millions of processing elements this monitoring technique can result in huge amounts of information. Monitoring long running applications is also challenging.

Therefore, monitoring everything in detail over millions of processing elements will not be a smart strategy to monitor future exascale applications. It will be much better to combine different strategies and techniques, i.e., using sampling and profiling approaches to get an overview of the application and using selective event tracing techniques to monitor specific functions, regions, and processing elements of interest in detail. In this paper, we focus on event-based monitoring and present existing and novel techniques to monitor and analyse specific parts of the application in detail.

2   Selective Monitoring

Selective monitoring is one component for a detailed performance analysis of exascale applications. The main intention is to reduce the amount of data without losing significant information. For an event-based monitoring approach there are basically two techniques that can be used to reach this goal, selective instrumentation (compile time filtering) and filtering at application runtime. Depending on the parallel paradigm and the corresponding instrumentation technique used, different selection mechanisms are available.

2.1   Compile Time Filtering

In contrast to runtime filtering, where the decision whether to profile or not is made during execution, compile time filtering makes this decision at compile time and thus decreases the runtime overhead.

By default, the selective monitoring capability of today's monitoring systems like Score-P [1], TAU [2], Extrae [3], and VampirTrace [4] mainly depend on the event-based automatic compiler instrumentation technique used.

With the exception of GNU and Intel, none the commonly used compilers in the HPC field support any kind of compile time filtering. And even the filtering capabilities of these two compilers are very limited. For other compilers like PGI and Cray there is only the possibility to exclude whole source files from the instrumentation by the monitoring system. Source-to-source instrumentors like PDT [5] and Opari [6] can also be executed on selected files by the monitoring system. In addition, PDT allows to specify lists of functions and regions that should be excluded from the source-to-source instrumentation. Binary instrumentor like DynInst [7] also allow to specify white-list and black-lists of functions that should be instrumented.

The support for sophisticated compile time filtering is desperately needed in the HPC community, especially for exascale applications. GCCs filtering capability is restricted to sub-string matching for the function and source file name. Imagine two functions, one is named foo the other barfoo. In case you want to filter foo, this also filters barfoo, rendering the filter useless.

Frameworks for code instrumentation like InterAspect [8], an aspect-oriented instrumentation framework for GCC plug-ins, can be used to replace the compiler instrumentation and use the available filtering features from the framework to extend it at will. The plug-ins are developed using the familiar vocabulary of Aspect-Oriented Programming (AOP) in which instrumentation is done using pointcuts (a set of join points, special points in the code). These plug-ins are then part of the GCC compiler and are executed in the code transformation phase of the compiler. A runtime filter typically is a piece of code that evaluates at program execution whether an event (function entry and exit) should be logged, normally using hooks provided by the compiler. With InterAspect, one can not only filter functions by name as is done by GNU or Intel, parameters of the function calls, the return type and so on can be included within the instrumentation process too. It is also possible to duplicate each functions body, instrument only the duplicate, and provide a runtime governor, who decides which of the two functions are executed. This yields reduced data overhead since only desired information is gathered with better reliability. Figures 1 and 2 illustrate the effect of runtime vs. compile time filtering. The benchmark used measures the performance of multiple matrix-matrix multiplication permutations. Beside these 7 functions of interest, the benchmark executes a lot of helper functions (i.e., timer accuracy, timer overhead, memory allocation/confusion, . . .). These functions aren't of interest but, in the case of runtime filtering, contain the instrumentation code plus the runtime filtering code. This alters the resulting function statistic of the main function when filtered with an runtime filter as shown in Fig. 1 because the instrumentation wastes time profiling unreported functions. The function statistic in Fig. 2 accurately reflect the distribution of the runtime for the 7 functions as it would look like without any instrumentation.

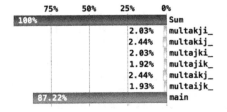

Fig. 1. Runtime filtering

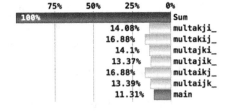

Fig. 2. Compile time filtering

2.2   Dynamic Runtime Filtering

Each of the before mentioned monitoring tools provides different strategies to filter functions at application runtime. Score-P and VampirTrace allow to exclude all functions from monitoring, record only the first n occurrences of a function, or record an interval of occurrences of a function. Extrae is able to start the recording after n occurrences of a global communication function or if a specific file exists. However, all strategies are applied on a global function-based context, i.e., each process uses the same runtime filtering rules, and there is actually no functionality to distinguish a function by different criteria.

To enable a more specific and dynamic runtime filtering, filter rules and specifications should be more flexible and context-dependent, i.e., depending on the temporal, spatial (processes, threads), and calling context. This means, that the filtering should be tailored to each processing element, to the calling context, and to specific phases/intervals of the application measurement.

The combination of selective instrumentation with temporal, spatial, and calling-context specific filtering at runtime will allow us to monitor applications in detail in more a dynamic and flexible way. For example, this may allow us to monitor specific iterations of an application and to disable the monitoring for the rest of the runtime.

2.3   Multi-Faceted Program Monitoring

The general work-flow of today's event-based monitoring is to instrument an application, to execute it multiple times at once (SPMD), and to record event information for each process. In general, this results in similar information about the application for each process. Within this context, the challenge of monitoring future exascale applications will be to handle the enormous amount of data with an high percentage of similar information while millions of processes or threads will be executed and monitored simultaneously. Dynamic runtime filtering (see Sect. 2.2) is able to reduce the amount of data but not to address the overhead issue introduced by entering and leaving an instrumented function and checking the corresponding filter rules. The monitoring overhead can be controlled using selective instrumentation techniques (see Sect. 2.1) to filter the to be monitored events by their parallel paradigm and name.

With the ability of modern MPI's to run MPMD programs, on either task or node basis, it is possible to execute different instrumented versions of the application simultaneously and to gain different level of details about the application on each process. This novel way of a selective event-based monitoring based on executing different instrumented versions of an application with a MPMD approach simultaneously in combination with dynamic filtering for each process is what we call **Multi-Faceted Program Monitoring**.

This strategy will allow us for example to monitor only a subset of processes like representatives of a class of similar processes instead of every process. For an exascale application this helps us to reduce the amount of data and to focus the monitoring on selected processes. One extreme case scenario would be to use the original unmodified application and one instrumented version of this application, to execute the instrumented version only on one selected node and on the other hundreds of thousand nodes the unmodified application will be executed. This scenario is beneficial if we know for example by using profiling approaches that processes of this selected node are the cause for performance bottlenecks and we want to monitor the runtime behaviour of theses processes in detail over time to detect the reason for the performance bottlenecks.

2.4   Example of Use

To demonstrate how event-based performance monitoring can benefit from the Multi-Faceted Program Monitoring approach, we monitored a tri-hybrid MPI/ OpenMP/CUDA version of Gromacs 4.6.5 [9] running on a Cray XC30 with four nodes, with each node hosting one MPI process with six OpenMP CPU threads and two GPU CUDA streams first with a traditional monitoring approach and after this with the Multi-Faceted Program Monitoring approach for 4000 iterations. For the traditional monitoring approach we used one instrumented version of Gromacs in such a way that MPI functions, OpenMP regions, CUDA kernels, and applications are monitored for every process. In contrast to the traditional approach we used three different instrumented versions of Gromacs for the Multi-Faceted Program Monitoring approach and executed these versions simultaneously as follows: On the first node we executed the version used for the traditional monitoring; on the second node we also used this version and combined it with a runtime filtering of selected application functions; on the third node we used a version that monitors MPI functions, OpenMP regions, CUDA kernel; and on the fourth node we monitored only MPI functions and CUDA kernels.

Figure 3 shows the colour-coded performance visualisation of Gromacs with the traditional monitoring approach with Vampir for an interval of 2.3 s. The monitored data per node ranges from 523 MByte to 1126 MByte. Figure 4 shows the colour-coded performance visualisation of Gromacs with the Multi-Faceted Program Monitoring approach with Vampir for the same interval. With this monitoring approach we were able to monitor the application in various level of detail on each node and to reduce the amount of data by 70.5 percent on the second node up to 97.2 percent on the fourth node.

3   Selective Visualisation

Besides selective monitoring, selective trace analysis and visualisation is a key prerequisite for a detailed exascale performance analysis. With limited screen resolution, only partial data or statistically aggregated data, e.g., clustering or wavelet analysis information, can be displayed at once. Therefore, to display detailed information of specific events, intervals or processing elements, the performance visualiser should be able to selectively load and analyse the corresponding trace data.

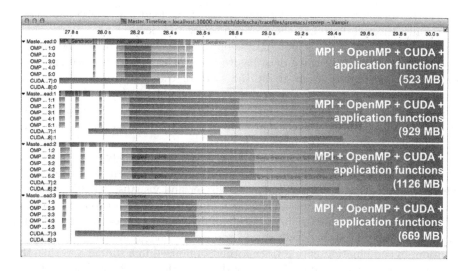

Fig. 3. Colour-coded performance visualisation of Gromacs monitored with the traditional monitoring approach running on a Cray XC30 with four nodes, with each node hosting one MPI process with six OpenMP CPU threads and two GPU CUDA streams for an interval of 2.3 s. On each process MPI functions, OpenMP regions, CUDA kernels, and application functions are monitored and the amount of data monitored per node ranges from 523 MByte to 1126 MByte.

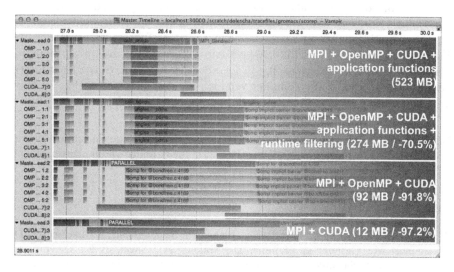

Fig. 4. Colour-coded performance visualisation of Gromacs monitored with the Multifaceted Program Monitoring approach running on a Cray XC30 with four nodes, with each node hosting one MPI process with six OpenMP CPU threads and two GPU CUDA streams for the same interval. On each node different level of details are monitored and the amount of data was reduced by 70.5 up to 97.2 percent.

The performance visualiser Vampir [4] allows to load and analyse spatially, temporally selected data, i.e., the user can select and deselect specific processes and threads for the analysis and analyse only selected phases of the monitoring run. For this, the native trace data has to be enriched with so-called snapshot information, i.e., information about the state of the application at a certain point of the measurement run, to enable a consistent stack view and a consistent message matching of the trace information. With a strategy presented in [10], we additionally ensure a correct matching of send or receive events even under the presence of missing MPI message events.

Another level of selective trace analysis could be the analysis of trace data dependent on the level of detail. Using information about the stack level and the duration of events, the performance analyser and visualiser could be able to regard or neglect performance information. This strategy will of course affect the inclusive and exclusive metric information of an event but allows to analyse and visualize different levels of detail (coarse grained vs. fine grained information). In addition, in combination with a trace format organized in a similar way, like the hierarchical in-memory buffers [11], or with knowledge about the distribution of events over the different stack levels, this selected level of detail strategy can be used to load, analyse, and visualise only a given percentage of the original monitored trace information.

4   Conclusion and Outlook

Selective monitoring and visualisation are key prerequisites for a detailed exascale performance analysis. We will therefore research the strategies and techniques presented in this paper in more detail in the near future. The instrumentation prototype created with InterAspect encourages us to develop a production quality GCC instrumentation plug-in for Score-P. It will have the least instrumentation overhead of any compiler vendor provided instrumentation we know of. Results for these measurements will be provided in the future.

Acknowledgment. This research has received funding from the European Community's Seventh Framework Programme (ICT-2011.9.13) under Grant Agreement no. 287703, cresta.eu.

References

1. Knüpfer, A., Rössel, C., an Mey, D., Biersdorff, S., Diethelm, K., Eschweiler, D., Geimer, M., Gerndt, M., Lorenz, D., Malony, A., Nagel, W.E., Oleynik, Y., Philippen, P., Saviankou, P., Schmidl, D., Shende, S., Tschüter, R., Wagner, M., Wesarg, B., Wolf, F.: Score-P: a joint performance measurement run-time infrastructure for Periscope, Scalasca, TAU, and Vampir. In: Brunst, H., Müller, M.S., Nagel, W.E., Resch, M.M. (eds.) Tools for High Performance Computing 2011, pp. 79–91. Springer, Heidelberg (2012)
2. Shende, S., Malony, A.D.: The TAU parallel performance system. Int. J. High Perform. Comput. Appl. **20**(2), 287–331 (2006). SAGE Publications

3. BSC: Extrae User guide manual for version 2.5.0 (2014). http://www.bsc.es/sites/default/files/public/computer_science/performance_tools/extrae-2.5.0-user-guide.pdf

4. Knüpfer, A., Brunst, H., Doleschal, J., Jurenz, M., Lieber, M., Mickler, H., Müller, M.S., Nagel, W.E.: The Vampir Performance analysis tool set. In: Tools for High Performance Computing, pp. 139–155 (2008)

5. Shende, S.S., Malony, A.D.: The tau parallel performance system. Int. J. High Perform. Comput. Appl. **20**, 287–331 (2006)

6. Mohr, B., Malony, A.D., Shende, S., Wolf, F.: Design and prototype of a performance tool interface for openmp. J. Supercomput. **23**, 105–128 (2002)

7. Buck, B., Hollingsworth, J.K.: An api for runtime code patching. Int. J. High Perform. Comput. Appl. **14**, 317–329 (2000)

8. Seyster, J., Dixit, K., Huang, X., Grosu, R., Havelund, K., Smolka, S.A., Stoller, S.D., Zadok, E.: Interaspect: aspect-oriented instrumentation with GCC. Formal Meth. Syst. Des. **41**, 295–320 (2012)

9. Hess, B., Kutzner, C., van der Spoel, D., Lindahl, E.: GROMACS 4: algorithms for highly efficient, load-balanced, and scalable molecular simulation. J. Chem. Theory Comput. **4**(3), 435–447 (2008). Please check and confirm the inserted year for reference [9]

10. Wagner, M., Doleschal, J., Nagel, W.E., Knüpfer, A.: Runtime message uniquification for accurate communication analysis on incomplete mpi event traces. In: Proceedings of the 20th European MPI Users' Group Meeting, EuroMPI 2013, pp. 123–128 (2013)

11. Wagner, M., Knüpfer, A., Nagel, W.E.: Hierarchical memory buffering techniques for an in-memory event tracing extension to the open trace format 2. In: 2013 42nd International Conference on Parallel Processing (ICPP), pp. 970–976 (2013)

Performance Analysis of Irregular Collective Communication with the Crystal Router Algorithm

Michael Schliephake[(✉)] and Erwin Laure

Department for High Performance Computing and Visualization and SeRC - Swedish E-Science Research Center, CSC School of Computer Science and Communication, KTH Royal Institute of Technology, 100 44 Stockholm, Sweden
{michs,erwinl}@kth.se

Abstract. In order to achieve exascale performance it is important to detect potential bottlenecks and identify strategies to overcome them. For this, both applications and system software must be analysed and potentially improved. The EU FP7 project *Collaborative Research into Exascale Systemware, Tools & Applications* (CRESTA) chose the approach to co-design advanced simulation applications and system software as well as development tools. In this paper, we present the results of a co-design activity focused on the simulation code NEK5000 that aims at performance improvements of collective communication operations. We have analysed the algorithms that form the core of NEK5000's communication module in order to assess its viability on recent computer architectures before starting to improve its performance. Our results show that the crystal router algorithm performs well in sparse, irregular collective operations for medium and large processor number but improvements for even larger system sizes of the future will be needed. We sketch the needed improvements, which will make the communication algorithms also beneficial for other applications that need to implement latency-dominated communication schemes with short messages. The latency-optimised communication operations will also become used in a runtime-system providing dynamic load balancing, under development within CRESTA.

Keywords: MPI · Collective operations · Performance tuning

1 Introduction

The development of applications showing exascale performance proves to be very challenging. On one side, it comprises efforts to scale today's numerical algorithms, system software, and development tools with proven methods as well as the refactoring of non-optimal code pieces that would become bottlenecks in runs at larger scale. On the other side, the development of exascale applications includes the search for qualitatively new approaches that reduce the computational complexity especially of algorithms with non-linear scaling for

© Springer International Publishing Switzerland 2015
S. Markidis and E. Laure (Eds.): EASC 2014, LNCS 8759, pp. 130–140, 2015.
DOI: 10.1007/978-3-319-15976-8_10

increasing processor counts. *Collaborative Research into Exascale Systemware, Tools & Applications* (CRESTA) is an EU FP7 project that concentrates on the study and solution of issues that are connected with the development towards exascale computing [1]. CRESTA chose an approach based on the co-design of advanced simulation applications and system software. The development of simulation codes has been flanked with the further development of necessary developer tools like parallel debuggers and performance analysis tools. CRESTA's co-design applications are running at the limits of available HPC computer installations while researchers create an ever-increasing demand for larger, respectively faster simulations and new application fields. This tension provides requirements and challenges for system software and tool developers. More demanding use cases can be used at the same time as test cases of new developments and are checkpoints to assess improvements though, for the time being still on current computers. Additionally, this approach provides general lessons usable in more simulation applications like those developed in the *Swedish e-Science Research Centre* (SeRC) as well as in the development of future software development tools [2].

In this paper, we present the results of a co-design activity focused on the simulation code NEK5000 that aims at performance improvements of collective communication operations. NEK5000 can be used for simulations of fluid flow, heat transfer and magnetohydrodynamics problems. It is an open-source code mainly developed at the Mathematics and Computer Science Division of the Argonne National Lab.

NEK5000 is a mature solver for incompressible Navier-Stokes equations. The numerical algorithm utilises high-order spatial discretisation with spectral elements and high-order semi-implicit time stepping for the calculations [12]. An important property of the algorithm is its fast convergence and the comparatively low complexity with respect to the number of grid points n. The complexity limits are for the discretisation at $O(n^6)$. The computational work and memory accesses only require costs of $O(n^4)$ and $O(n^3)$ respectively [13]. The application has won the Gordon Bell Prize in 1999 and many simulation projects on different HPC computer installations show its scalability up to one million cores. Despite its excellent scaling behaviour, the crystal router still exposes areas for improvements. Our on-going co-design activity aims at implementations of effective collective communication operations for large-scale runs as well as the reduction of the communication volume using a hybrid parallelisation scheme [9].

In this paper, we present an analysis of the crystal router algorithm, which is the base of NEK5000's central communication module. It will allow to use this solution as a base for the implementation of alternative, improved collective communication operations. We identify bottlenecks and sketch strategies to overcome these. These new collective operations can be used also in other applications as well as a building block in a runtime-system, which helps to dynamically improve load balancing [8]. The remainder of this paper is organized as follows: After a discussion of related work in Sect. 2 we describe the functionality of the crystal router in Sect. 3. Benchmark results will be presented and discussed in Sect. 4. Section 5 concludes the paper with an outlook on future work.

2   Related Work

Sur et. al. developed efficient routines for personalized all-to-all exchange on Infiniband clusters [10]. They use Infiniband RDMA operations combined with hypercube algorithms and achieved speedup factors of three for short messages of 32 B on 16 nodes.

Li et. al. use Infiniband's virtual lanes for the improvement of collective MPI operations in multi-core clusters [6]. These virtual lanes are used for balancing multiple send requests active at the same time and to increase the throughput for small messages. This implementation showed a performance improvement of 10–20 %.

Li et. al. analyse the influence of synchronisation messages on the communication performance. Those messages are used in collective operations to control of the exchange of large messages [7]. They found that contention of synchronisation messages accounts for a large portion of the operation's overall latency. Their algorithm optimises the exchange and achieved improvements of 25 % for messages between 32 and 64 kB length.

Tu et. al. propose a model of the memory-hierarchy in multi-core clusters that uses horizontal and vertical levels [11]. Their experimental results show that this model is capable to predict the communication costs of collective operations more accurately than it was possible before. They developed a methodology to optimize collective operations and demonstrated it with the implementation of a multi-core aware broadcast operation.

3   Functionality of the Crystal Router

The crystal router as developed by Fox et. al. [4] is an algorithm that allows sending messages of arbitrary length between arbitrary nodes in a hypercube network. It is advantageous especially in irregular applications where the exact nature of the communication is not known before it occurs or where the message emergence changes dynamically.

Communication operations in hypercube networks are often implemented by routing algorithms that iterate over the dimensions of the cube and execute in each step one point-to-point communication operation with the partner node at the other end of the respective edge. As explained for example in [5], the result of the binary xor function with the processor numbers of sender and receiver node as arguments provides a routing path that can be used to transport the message. Therefore, messages can be delivered in algorithms following this pattern from each node to each other node in at most d communication steps where d is the dimensionality of the hypercube network. In our implementation, we interpret MPI processes as nodes of a hypercube network and use MPI ranks as processor numbers.

It has been proven that such a choice of paths provides load balancing in the communication of several typical applications as well as it is optimal if all processors are used in a load balanced way [5]. The crystal router has been developed to handle one typical situation of processes in hypercube networks. In each process, there is a set of messages, which must be sent to other processes. Destination processes expect messages, but they know neither exactly how many messages will arrive nor from which processes they will be sent. Nevertheless, the communication happens for many algorithms typically in communication phases between computations in a time-synchronised manner. One example is the irregularity in the communication of molecular dynamics algorithms. The real amount of data that has to be communicated between neighbouring subdomains is not known before the data exchange itself. Another example of slightly irregular communication can be found in finite element calculations where the meshes must be decomposed over several processors. This decomposition will be perfect only to a certain degree. Therefore, the communication between the nodes holding the different subdomains will show some load-imbalance.

Algorithm 1 explains how the transport of messages between arbitrary processes works. First, all messages are stored in a buffer for outgoing messages of the sender process (msg_out). During the iteration over the different channels (i.e. the bits of rank numbers), some messages will be transmitted in each iteration step according to their routing path. For that, those messages that must be transferred through a certain channel will be copied from msg_out to a common transfer buffer (msg_next). The buffer msg_next of each process will be exchanged through the active channel of the current iteration step with the respective buffer of a partner process. Thereafter, all messages that had to be routed from this partner over this channel can be found in msg_next. They will be inspected there. Messages that are addressed to the receiving process will be copied into the buffer for incoming messages (msg_in) from where they can be accessed by the application code later. Messages that have to be forwarded further in one of the following iteration steps will be kept and put into msg_out.

Algorithm 1. Pseudocode of the crystal router algorithm, adapted from [4].

```
begin crystal_router
    declare buffer msg_out;  /* buffer for messages to send    */
    declare buffer msg_in;   /* buffer for received messages   */
    declare buffer msg_next; /* buffer for messages to send    */
                             /* in the next communication step */

    for each msg in msg_out  do
        if dest_rank(msg) == myrank  then
            copy msg into msg_in;
    end for
    for each dimension of the hypercube i = 0,...,d-1  do
        for each message msg in msg_out  do
            if (dest_rank(msg)&myrank)^2^i  then
```

```
            copy  msg into msg_next;
        end for
        exchange buffer msg_next with process(rank == myrank^2^i);
        for each message msg in msg_next  do
            if dest_rank(msg) == myrank  then
                copy msg into msg_in;
            if  msg needs to be routed further  then
                copy msg into msg_out;
        end for
    end for
end crystal_router
```

Summarizing, this algorithm guarantees message delivery between arbitrary processes within d steps where d is the dimensionality of the hypercube network. Furthermore, it maximises the message lengths for each communication step by bundling messages that have a segment of their routing paths in common, provided that the necessary buffers can be allocated with a sufficient size.

4   Performance Analysis of the Crystal Router

We developed a synthetic benchmark for the analysis of the original crystal router algorithm. Its design has been based on the communication pattern in NEK5000. There, elements usually have 26 neighbour elements. Each of them could be located in a different process, i.e. processes have to exchange data with at least 26 neighbours due to spatial domain decomposition. The element distribution logic tries to keep neighbouring elements in processes on nodes near to each other, but, it is also possible that some elements will be placed on distant nodes. Our benchmark allows to define the number of communication partners of each process as well as their distance in form of a stride that will be used to select them. Selected nodes will exchange messages during the benchmark run. The overall number of spectral elements per node, which corresponds to a certain message length, could be adapted in order to test strong scaling. In the strong scaling case, the volume-surface ratio of the elements located in one process causes a communication amount per node that is proportional to the number p of processes with $O(p^{-2/3})$. The aggregated communication of the job then follows the function $O(p^{1/3})$. The number of elements as well as the amount of communication per process remains constant for weak scaling. The aggregated communication of the parallel job will be limited by $O(p)$ though.

The measurements have been done on KTH's system Lindgren. It is a Cray XE6 installation equipped with two AMD Opteron 6172 processors ("magny core") and 32 GB RAM per compute node. It has a size of 1516 nodes, i.e. 36384 cores, and provides 305 TFLOPS peak performance. The system interconnect is a Cray Gemini network with a 3D-torus topology [3].

The first benchmark shows the performance of the crystal router for different message lenghts and numbers of nodes in comparison to the standard

MPI library of Lindgren. The benchmarked operation is a personalized all-to-all communication that is provided as MPI_Alltoallv. The crystal router based implementation is called Cr_Alltoallv. The benchmark has been setup in such a way, that each MPI process communicates with its 26 nearest neighbours. The results for runs with 256 and 512 processes are shown in Fig. 1. The results for 1024 and 2048 processes are shown in Fig. 2. Finally, Fig. 3 provides results for 4096 and 8192 processes.

The crystal router based implementation Cr_Alltoallv is much faster than MPI_Alltoallv in runs of all sizes especially for short, latency-bound messages. For example, $85\,\mu s$ are needed for a Cr_Alltoallv operation that lets each rank exchange 8 Bytes with its partner processes in a run with 256 processes. The operation takes $273\,\mu s$ for 8192 processes. The ratio of these times is 1 : 3.2. The same operation needs $3\,227\,\mu s$ for 256 processes and $187\,000\,\mu s$ with 8192 processes with the function MPI_Alltoallv. The ratio of the times is 1 : 58. This result demonstrates that sparse communication patterns involving all processes of a parallel program can be realised efficiently by the crysral router.

The speed advantage of the crystal router becomes smaller for longer messages. The speeds of the MPI system function and of the crystal router are almost equal for the longest messages of 128 kB in the smallest test of 256 processes. The speed difference increases for this message length with an increasing processor count and reaches a factor of 19 for the largest run utilising 8192 processes.

Furthermore, the benchmarks show that the number of communication partners respectively the size of the stride do not noticeably influence the duration of the operation for the MPI system function. The crystal router implementation contrastingly is more sensitive to these parameters. Figure 4 shows measurements for a varying stride length utilizing 2048 processes and transmitting messages

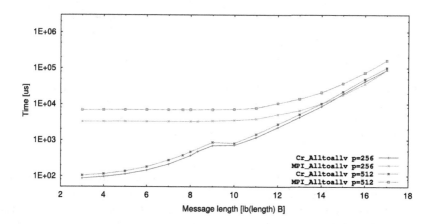

Fig. 1. Benchmark of personalized all-to-all communication implemented with the crystal router based function Cr_Alltoallv and the MPI function MPI_Alltoallv. Each process sends and receives data from 26 neighbouring processes. The measurements have been executed with 256 respectively 512 processes.

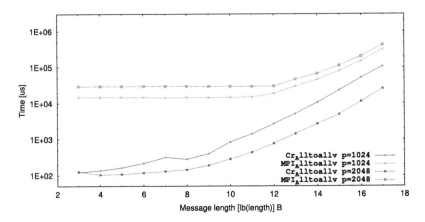

Fig. 2. Benchmark of personalized all-to-all communication implemented with the crystal router based function `Cr_Alltoallv` and the MPI function `MPI_Alltoallv`. Each process sends and receives data from 26 neighbouring processes. The measurements have been executed with 1024 respectively 2048 processes.

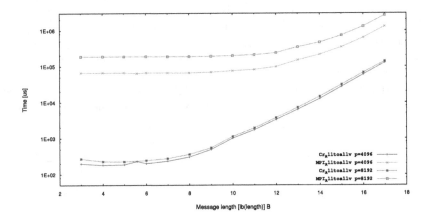

Fig. 3. Benchmark of personalized all-to-all communication implemented with the crystal router based function `Cr_Alltoallv` and the MPI function `MPI_Alltoallv`. Each process sends and receives data from 26 neighbouring processes. The measurements have been executed with 4096 respectively 8192 processes.

of 8 resp. 512 byte length. The crystal router needs an increasing runtime for increasing strides. This reflects that the increasing stride length between the communications causes increasing data amounts that must be transfered the processes that are located on other numa nodes, on other sockets and on other nodes. For example, the time needed for the communication operation with a stride of 24 (i.e. each process communicates only with processes that reside on other nodes) is compared to a 1-stride 59 % longer for messages of 8 byte length, and it needs 51 % more time for messages of 512 byte length. Such a systematic trend could not be observed with the MPI routine. Its variability is clearly smaller than 10 %.

Figure 5 presents a benchmark that has been executed with 256 processes. Here, the number of communication partners of the processes has been varied. The MPI system routine again does not show significant variations in their runtime. The crystal router implementation needs longer runtimes for an increasing number of communication partners per process. The result reflects the increasing communication volume that has to be processed by the constant number of processors.

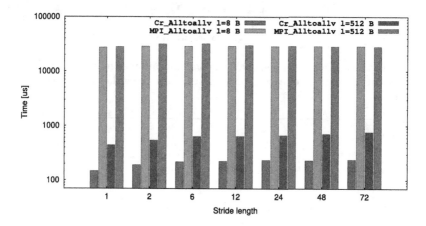

Fig. 4. Benchmark of all-to-all personalized communication as function of the distance between communicating processes in the process list (stride). The measurement has been executed with 256 processes.

Finally, the evaluation with respect to weak scaling in Fig. 6 demonstrates that Cr_Alltoallv scales very uniformly for short messages. Its scaling behaviour is noticeable better than that of MPI_Alltoallv.

Our analysis shows that the crystal router algorithm is beneficial for medium-sized and large parallel programs. It can unfold its capabilities compared to the function MPI_Alltoallv especially in situations with sparse communication patterns and for large processor counts. Its uniform scaling into ranges of large processor counts indicates that there are no effects of performance degeneration in the algorithm itself and that it can be a viable choice for the implementation of collective communication operations. However, several improvements of the original algorithm are needed, particularly

– the reduction of data copies,
– the exploitation of multiple communication paths, and
– the overlapping of data transfers with the processing of the messages.

Specifically on Cray systems, the exploitation of multiple communication paths and the overlapping of data transfers with the process-internal message

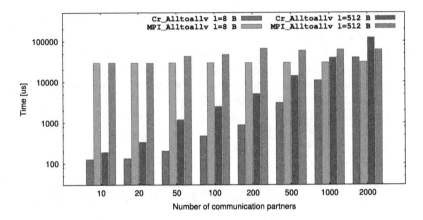

Fig. 5. Benchmark of all-to-all personalized communication as function of the number of communication partners of each process. The measurement has been executed with 256 processes.

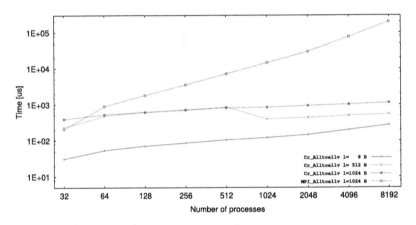

Fig. 6. Weak-scaling of all-to-all personalized communication with `Cr_Alltoallv` for message lengths of 8, 512, and 1024 B. For comparison the scaling of `MPI_Alltoallv` for a message length of 1024 B has been given.

handling will provide significant performance improvements. The 3D-torus connects to each Gemini chip with several links. The Block Transfer Engine (BTE) of the Gemini chip allows to offload the transfer of larger messages from the CPU. Therefore, a refatcoring of the original algorithm using these hardware capabilities will extend the range of its applicability.

5   Conclusions and Future Work

We evaluated the original crystal router algorithm in an implementation of a personalized all-to-all communication on a recent computer architecture. It shows a superior exchange performance especially for short messages up to 4 kilobyte and parallel runs of medium and large sizes. It showed furthermore a uniform scaling over the whole range of job sizes. This is possible because it bundles short messages into larger packages that will be transferred at once. The influence of latency is reduced in that way, and MPI library optimisations with respect to the bandwidth of larger message lengths become useable for shorter messages too. The crystal router is sensitive slightly to the distance of the communicating processes and to a larger extend to the number of communication partners per process, i.e. the degree of sparsity. These comparatively small variations and the high overall efficiency that is achieved at the same time are an effect of the algorithm's properties. The message bundling and the algorithm design guarantee the message delivery within a fixed number of communication steps. Finally, the hypercube algorithm involves all nodes equally into the transport of messages during each communication step.

Our benchmarks confirm that the crystal router algorithm could be used efficiently also on modern computer architectures, however, to make it ready for exascale, the efficiency on higher processor counts needs to be improved furthermore. We have sketched key aspects of these improvements, particularly the reduction of data copying and the use of multiple network connections. These improvements will make the crystal router based communication substrate a viable choice for exascale applications.

Acknowledgements. We would like to thank for the support of this work through the projects *Collaborative Research into Exascale Systemware, Tools & Applications* (CRESTA) and *Swedish e-Science Research Centre* (SeRC).

References

1. EU FP7 project CRESTA. http://cresta-project.eu/
2. Swedish e-Science Research Centre (SeRC). http://www.e-science.se/
3. Alverson, R., Roweth, D., Kaplan, L.: The gemini system interconnect. In: 2010 IEEE 18th Annual Symposium on High Performance Interconnects (HOTI), pp. 83–87, 18–20 August 2010
4. Fox, G.C., et al.: Solving Problems on Concurrent Processors: General Techniques and Regular Problems. Prentice Hall, Englewood Cliffs (1988)
5. Grama, A.: Introduction to Parallel Computing. Addison-Wesley, Harlow (2003)
6. Li, B., Huo, Z., Zhang, P., Meng, D.: Multiple virtual lanes-aware MPI collective communication in multi-core clusters. In: 2009 International Conference on High Performance Computing (HiPC), pp. 304–311, 16-19 December 2009
7. Li, Q., Huo, Z., Sun, N.: Optimizing MPI alltoall communication of large messages in multicore clusters. In: 2011 12th International Conference on Parallel and Distributed Computing, Applications and Technologies (PDCAT), pp. 257–262, 20–22 October 2011
8. Schliephake, M., Aguilar, X., Laure, E.: Design and implementation of a runtime system for parallel numerical simulations on large-scale clusters. In: Procedia Computer Science, Proceedings of the International Conference on Computational Science, ICCS 2011, vol. 4, pp. 2105–2114 (2011)

9. Schliephake, M., Laure, E.: Towards improving the communication performance of CRESTA's co-design application NEK5000. In: High Performance Computing, Networking, Storage and Analysis (SCC), 2012 SC Companion, pp. 669–674, 10–16 November 2012
10. Sur, S., Hyun-Wook, J., Panda, D.K.: Efficient and scalable all-to-all personalized exchange for InfiniBand-based clusters. In: ICPP 2004, 2004 International Conference on Parallel Processing, vol. 1, pp. 275–282, 15–18 August 2004
11. Tu, B., Fan, J., Zhan, J., Zhao, X.: Performance analysis and optimization of MPI collective operations on multi-core clusters. J. Supercomput. **60**(1), 141–162 (2012)
12. Tufo, H.M., Fscher, P.F.: Terascale spectral element algorithms and implementations, Gordon Bell prize paper. In: Proceedings of the ACM/IEEE SC99 Conference on High Performance Networking and Computing. IEEE Computer Society, CDROM (1999)
13. Tufo, H.M., Fischer, P.F.: Fast parallel direct solvers for coarse grid problems. J. Par. & Dist. Comput. **61**, 151–177 (2001)

The Architecture of Vistle, a Scalable Distributed Visualization System

Martin Aumüller[(✉)]

HLRS, University of Stuttgart, Stuttgart, Germany
aumueller@hlrs.de

Abstract. Vistle is a scalable distributed implementation of the visualization pipeline. Modules are realized as MPI processes on a cluster. Within a node, different modules communicate via shared memory. TCP is used for communication between clusters.

Vistle targets especially interactive visualization in immersive virtual environments. For low latency, a combination of parallel remote and local rendering is possible.

Keywords: Distributed visualization · Architecture · Hybrid parallel visualization · In-situ visualization · Virtual reality

1 Overview

Vistle [10] is a modular and extensible implementation of the visualization pipeline [8]. It integrates simulations on supercomputers, post-processing and parallel interactive visualization in immersive virtual environments. It is designed to work distributed across multiple clusters. The objective is to provide a highly scalable system, exploiting data, task and pipeline parallelism in hybrid shared and distributed memory environments with acceleration hardware. Domain decompositions used during simulation shall be reused for visualization as far as possible for minimizing data transfer and I/O.

A Vistle work flow consists of several processing modules, each of which is a parallel MPI program that uses OpenMP within nodes. Shared memory is used for transferring data between modules within a single node, MPI within a cluster, TCP across clusters.

2 Related Work

Data parallelism is available in several distributed systems based on the visualization pipeline: VisIt [2] and ParaView [13] rely on algorithms implemented by VTK [12] for many of their modules, while EnSight [3] has dedicated implementations. They all implement a client-server architecture, which only allows for restricted distributed processing: data objects can travel from one remote cluster server to a local display client system, but they cannot be routed between

© Springer International Publishing Switzerland 2015
S. Markidis and E. Laure (Eds.): EASC 2014, LNCS 8759, pp. 141–147, 2015.
DOI: 10.1007/978-3-319-15976-8_11

remote servers in an arbitrary order. Modules share a single address space on each node, which allows for embedding the complete visualization tool within the simulation application [15].

COVISE [16], the system we use currently, implements a fully distributed visualization pipeline: modules running on arbitrary systems can be chained together in any order. Each module is mapped to a separate operating system process. Data objects to be transferred to other modules are created in shared memory. They are transferred as needed to other systems transparently for the module programmer. Because of its multi-process architecture, task parallelism is inherent to the system. The most significant short-coming is the lack data-parallelism in distributed memory systems. COVISE has a strong focus on simulation steering, visualization and interaction in immersive virtual environments and supports collaboration between desktop and VR systems. Its render component OpenCOVER [11] builds on OpenSceneGraph.

3   Process Model

In Vistle, modules in the visualization pipeline are realized as individual MPI processes. `MPI_Comm_spawn_multiple` is used for controlling on which hosts they are started: in order for the shared memory mechanism to work, equivalent ranks of different processes have to be placed on the same host. But as this requirement for starting modules has proven to be difficult to realize in a portable manner with MPI, we are looking into alternatives for launching modules. One approach could be to spawn independent MPI jobs on the same nodes via `mpirun`. Figure 1 shows the process layout within a cluster.

The decision for multiple processes instead of multiple threads was made in order to decouple MPI communication in different stages of the pipeline without requiring a multi-thread aware MPI implementation.

Within individual nodes, OpenMP is used to exploit all available cores. We work on implementing the most important algorithms with the parallel building blocks supplied by Thrust [5] in order to achieve code and performance portability across OpenMP and CUDA accelerators. We hope that this reimplementation provides speed-ups for unstructured meshes of the same magnitude as has been achieved in PISTON [7] for structured grids.

4   Data Management

All data objects are created in shared memory managed by Boost. Interprocess [1]. This minimizes the communication overhead and data replication necessary for Vistle's multi-process model. As the function pointers stored in the virtual function table of C++ classes are valid only within the address space of a single process, virtual methods cannot be called for objects residing in shared memory. For the class hierarchy of shared memory data objects, there is a parallel hierarchy of proxy accessor objects, as shown in Fig. 2. Polymorphic behavior is

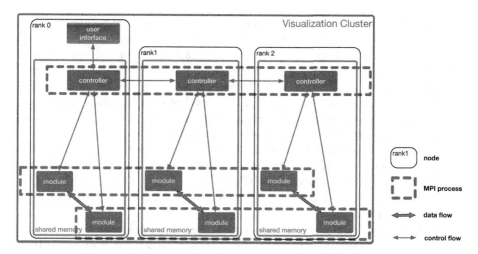

Fig. 1. Process layout, control flow and data flow within a single cluster: controller and modules are realized as MPI processes. Within a node, shared memory queues are used to route control messages through the controller; if necessary, they are routed via MPI through rank 0 of the controller to other ranks. Down-stream modules retrieve their input data from shared memory after being passed an object handle.

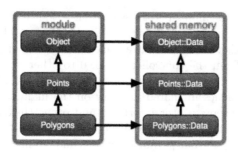

Fig. 2. Parallel class hierarchies for data objects residing in shared memory and accessor objects providing polymorphic behavior for modules.

restored by creating a corresponding proxy object within each process accessing a shared memory object. Life time of data objects is managed with reference counting. Caching of input objects for modules is implemented by simply keeping a reference to the objects.

The most important component of data objects are scalar arrays. They provide an interface compatible with STL's `vector` [6]. As an optimization for the common case of storing large arrays of scalar values, they are not initialized during allocation, as most often these default values would have to be overwritten immediately. These arrays are reference counted individually, such that shallow copies of data objects are possible and data arrays can be referenced from several data objects. This allows to e. g. reuse the coordinate array for both an unstructured volume grid and a corresponding boundary surface.

Data objects are created by modules, modification of data objects is not possible after they are published to other modules. The only exception to this rule is that any module can attach other objects to arbitrary objects. This is used to tie them to acceleration structures that can be reused across modules.

Data objects can be transmitted between nodes, but we try to avoid this overhead: we assume that in general the overhead of load balancing is not warranted as most visualization algorithms are fast and as the imbalances vary with the parameterization of the algorithm (e. g. iso value).

Objects carry metadata such as their name, source module, age, simulation time, simulation iteration and the number of the partition for domain decomposed data. Additionally, textual attributes can be attached to objects. This provides flexibility to e. g. manage hierarchic object groups or collections and to attach shaders to objects.

The hierarchy of data object classes comprises object types for unstructured grids, structured grids and collections of polygons and triangles, lines and points, the celltree [4] for accelerated cell search as well as scalar and vector data mapped onto these geometric structures. Users can extend the system with their own data types.

5   Control Flow and Message System

The central instance for managing the execution is the controller. Its main task is to handle events and manage control flow between modules. Messages for this purpose are rather small and have a fixed maximum size. MPI is used for transmitting them from the controller's rank 0 to other ranks. Within a rank, they are forwarded using shared memory message queues. The controller polls MPI and message queues in shared memory on the main thread. TCP is used for communicating them to user interfaces and other clusters. They are used to launch modules, trigger their execution, announce the availability of newly created data objects, transmit parameter values and communicate the execution state of a module.

Work flow descriptions are stored as Python scripts and are interpreted by the controller.

6   Modules

Modules are implemented by deriving from the module base class. During construction, a module should define its input and output ports as well as its parameters. For every tuple of objects received at its inputs, the compute() method of a module is called. By default, compute() is only invoked on the node where the data object has been received. In order to avoid synchronization overhead, MPI communication is only possible if a module explicitly opts in to parallel invocation of compute() on all ranks. If only a final reduction operation has to be performed after all blocks of a data set have been processed, a reduce() method can be implemented by modules. Compared to parallel invocation of compute(), this has lower synchronization overhead.

7   User Interfaces

User interfaces attach to or detach from a Vistle session dynamically at run-time. User interfaces connect to the controller's rank 0. For attaching to sessions started as a batch job on a system with limited network connectivity, the controller will connect to a proxy at a known location, where user interfaces can attach to instead. Upon connection, the current state of the session is communicated to the user interface. From then on, the state is tracked by observing Vistle messages that induce state changes. An arbitrary number of UIs can be attached at any time, thus facilitating simple collaboration. Graphical and command line/scripting user interfaces can be mixed at will. Their state always remains synchronized.

Graphical UIs provide an explicit representation of data flow: this makes the configured visualization pipeline easy to understand.

8   Rendering

Vistle is geared towards immersive virtual environments, where low latency is very important. For rendering, Vistle implements a plug-in for OpenCOVER. Visualization parameters can be manipulated from within the virtual environment. Large data sets can be displayed with sort-last parallel rendering and depth compositing implemented using IceT [9]. To facilitate access to remote HPC resources, a combination of local and parallel remote rendering called remote hybrid rendering [14] is available to decouple interaction from remote rendering. There is also a ray casting based backend renderer running entirely on the CPU, which enables access to remote resources without GPUs.

9   First Results

Performance of the system was evaluated with the visualization of the simulation of a pump turbine. The simulation was conducted by the Institute of Fluid Mechanics and Hydraulic Machinery at the University of Stuttgart with Open-FOAM on 128 processors. Accordingly, the data set was decomposed into 128 blocks. This also limits the amount of parallelism that can be reached. Figure 3 shows runtime and parallel efficiency. Isosurface extraction is interactive at rates of more than $20/s$ and runtime does not increase until full parallelism is reached. While this suggests that the approach is suitable for in-situ visualization, the impact on the performance of a simulation will have to be assessed specifically for each case: often, the simulation will have to be suspended while its state is captured, the visualization might compete for memory with the simulation, and the visualization will claim processor time slices from the simulation as it will be scheduled on the same cores. However, these costs are only relevant when in-situ visualization is actively used, as Vistle's modular design requires only a small component for interfacing with the visualization tool to remain in memory all the time.

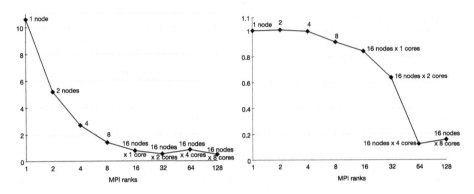

Fig. 3. Isosurface extraction on 13 timesteps of 5.8 million moving unstructured cells, runtime in s (left), parallel efficiency (right): runtime does not increase significantly until the number of ranks for the original simulation is reached. Extraction happens at interactive rates.

10 Current Status and Future Work

Not all features described here are already implemented. The most significant gap is the lack of most distributed features: only user interfaces and display modules can run remotely. Also, support for structured grids is still missing.

Current projects are the handling of halo cells in order to support algorithms which require data from neighboring cells. The next mile stones that we aim to achieve are to couple the system to OpenFOAM and to provide the infrastructure for algorithms which require tight coupling between the MPI processes of a module and, building on that, the implementation of a particle tracer for decomposed data sets that are spread across the nodes of a cluster. Additionally, the scalability of the system will be improved by making better use of OpenMP and acceleration hardware.

Acknowledgments. This work has been supported in part by the CRESTA project that has received funding from the European Community's Seventh Framework Programme (ICT-2011.9.13).

References

1. Abrahams, D., et al.: BOOST C++ Libraries. http://www.boost.org. Accessed 28 Jan 2014
2. Ahern, S., Childs, H., Brugger, E., Whitlock, B., Meredith, J.: VisIt: an end-user tool for visualizing and analyzing very large data. In: Proceedings of SciDAC (2011)
3. Frank, R., Krogh, M.F.: The EnSight visualization application. In: Bethel, E.W., Childs, H., Hansen, C. (eds.) High Performance Visualization-Enabling Extreme-Scale Scientific Insight, pp. 429–442. Chapman & Hall/CRC, Salt Lake City (2012)
4. Garth, C., Joy, K.I.: Fast, memory-efficient cell location in unstructured grids for visualization. IEEE Trans. Vis. Comput. Graph. **16**(6), 1541–1550 (2010)

5. Hoberock, J., Bell, N.: Thrust: A Parallel Template Library (2010). http://thrust. github.io/, version 1.7.0. Accessed 28 Jan 2014
6. Josuttis, N.M.: The C++ Standard Library. A Tutorial and Reference, 2nd edn. Addison-Wesley Professional, Boston (2012)
7. Lo, L.T., Ahrens, J., Sewell, C.: PISTON: a portable cross-platform framework for data-parallel visualization operators. In: EGPGV, pp. 11–20 (2012)
8. Moreland, K.: A survey of visualization pipelines. IEEE Trans. Vis. Comput. Graph. **19**(3), 367–378 (2013). http://ieeexplore.ieee.org/xpl/articleDetails.jsp?tp =&arnumber=6212499&contentType=Journals+%26+Magazines&matchBoolean %3Dtrue%26rowsPerPage%3D30%26searchField%3DSearch_All%26queryText%- 3D%28p_Title%3A%22a+survey+of+visualization+pipelines%22%29
9. Moreland, K., Kendall, W., Peterka, T., Huang, J.: An image compositing solution at scale. In: 2011 International Conference for High Performance Computing, Networking, Storage and Analysis (SC), pp. 1–10 (2011)
10. Niebling, F., Aumüller, M., Kimble, S., Kopf, C., Woessner, U.: Vistle Repository on GitHub. https://github.com/vistle/vistle. Accessed 28 Jan 2014
11. Rantzau, D., Lang, U.: A scalable virtual environment for large scale scientific data analysis. Future Gener. Comput. Syst.-Int. J. Grid Comput. Theory Methods Appl. **14**(3–4), 215–222 (1998)
12. Schroeder, W., Martin, K., Lorensen, B.: The Visualization Toolkit. An Object-Oriented Approach to 3D Graphics. Kitware Inc., Clifton Park (2006)
13. Squillacote, A.: The Paraview Guide. Kitware Inc., Clifton Park (2008)
14. Wagner, C., Flatken, M., Chen, F., Gerndt, A., Hansen, C.D., Hagen, H.: Interactive hybrid remote rendering for multi-pipe powerwall systems. In: Geiger, C., Herder, J., Vierjahn, T. (eds.) Virtuelle und Erweiterte Realität - 9. Workshop der GI-Fachgruppe VR/AR, pp. 155–166. Shaker Verlag, Aachen (2012)
15. Whitlock, B., Favre, J.M., Meredith, J.S.: Parallel in situ coupling of simulation with a fully featured visualization system. In: EGPGV, pp. 101–109, April 2011
16. Wierse, A., Lang, U., Rühle, R.: A system architecture for data-oriented visualization. In: Lee, J.P., Grinstein, Georges G. (eds.) Visualization-WS 1993. LNCS, vol. 871, pp. 148–159. Springer, Heidelberg (1994). http://www.springerlink.com/index/10.1007/BFb0021151

Author Index

Printed in the United States
By Bookmasters